Liberated Traditionalism

Liberated Traditionalism

Men & Women In Balance

RONALD & BEVERLY ALLEN

MULTNOMAH · PRESS

Portland, Oregon 97266

Other books by Ronald B. Allen:
Praise! A Matter of Life and Breath
Worship: Rediscovering the Missing Jewel
    (with Gordon Borror)
Praise: The Response to All of Life
When Song Is New: Understanding the Kingdom
    in the Psalms
Abortion: When Does Life Begin?
The Majesty of Man: The Dignity of Being Human
Imagination: God's Gift of Wonder
Lord of Song

Edited by Rodney L. Morris
Cover design and illustration by Britt Taylor Collins

LIBERATED TRADITIONALISM
© 1985 by Multnomah Press
Portland, Oregon 97266

Printed in the United States of America

Library of Congress Cataloging in Publication Data

Allen, Ronald Barclay.
    Liberated traditionalism.

    Includes bibliographical references and indexes.
    1. Women and religion.   2. Women in the Bible.
3. Feminism—Religious aspects.   4. Sex role.
I. Allen, Beverly.   II. Morris, Rodney L.   III. Title.
HQ1393.A43   1985   305.4'2   85-8960
ISBN 0-88070-112-9

85   86   87   88   89   90   91   –   10   9   8   7   6   5   4   3   2   1

To each other,
On the twenty-fifth anniversary
of our love.

Contents

Introduction

Women and men.

Simple words, no longer simple.
New order, new complexities.
Tradition and transition.

The last couple of decades have brought enormous societal pressures for change in Western culture. Particularly boggling are the forces for changes in the way we relate to each other as women and men.

These pressures for change in the relationships between the sexes have produced varied responses.

> Some women are jubilant at the advances they have made, and are more aggressive than ever in new agendas.
>
> Others are angry at what is happening in general and are determined to resist change in any form.
>
> Many people are simply confused. Bewilderment clutches both the new woman as well as the old-fashioned woman. And men are perhaps the most confused of all.

We Christians live in a new world. We are not yet comfortable. We don't feel at home at all. Where in this new world are thoughts of the values of tradition, of the imperatives of Scripture, of the pleasure of the Lord?

New words and manners press themselves upon us as we become sensitized to new perceptions of our humanity. Some of these issues are commonplace matters relating to the gentilities of the past. Gentlemen may wonder what the response will be as they reach out to open a door or hold a chair for a lady. Other issues make the commonplace uncommon. How does a hostess address an envelope to an unmarried couple or introduce someone's "significant other"?

Both major new questions and serious old problems arise as well. What are God's intentions for our relationships as women and men today? Have God's desires for us changed? Or did we misunderstand all along what his desires really were? What happens to biblical submission in a unisex society? Do these questions really matter?

Christians in particular question the new cultural pressures. Believers through the ages have ever had to wrestle with the clash of faith and culture. The specifics may be new, but the battle is as old as the faith.

Right-thinking Christians never wish to succumb to the pressures of the world to be pressed into its image and lose their distinctions from that world as pilgrims, as citizens of another kingdom.

Reflective Christians also do not wish to confuse their own merely traditional cultural norms with genuine biblical imperatives, and wind up resisting the good changes that the Spirit of God may be bringing into our lives from a variety of sources.

In this book we seek to present an approach to the relationship of women and men that is thoughtfully biblical and sensitively responsive to current issues. We do not wish to parrot old lines merely because they have been said before by many believers, nor do we wish to echo the latest activist refrain just because it is said so shrilly or sounds so chic.

As we have worked on writing this book, we have been asked by friends and acquaintances what our basic approach will be. We have decided to term our approach *liberated traditionalism*, and hope that this unlikely association of words will spur your interest in reading further.

The listing of Ron's name before Bev's on the title page might be regarded as a vestige of patriarchalism. (These things die hard.) It means in fact that the principal final writing was done by Ron, but Bev assisted, contributed, and collaborated substantially all along the way. Likely our next book together will have our names reversed.

We are doubly grateful to Multnomah Press for the trust given to the two of us to do this book together for the Critical Concern Books imprint. To our publisher, John Van Diest, and our editor, Rod Morris, we express our profound appreciation.

May God receive glory from women and men who read this book!

PART 1

FACING THE CRISIS
OF THE SEXES

What are little boys made of, made of?
What are little boys made of?
Frogs and snails and puppy-dogs' tails;
That's what little boys are made of.

What are little girls made of, made of?
What are little girls made of?
Sugar and spice and all things nice,
That's what little girls are made of.
Mother Goose

Chapter 1

A Question of Gender

A *rchie Bunker was supposed to have been a joke.* Norman Lear's long-running television program, "All in the Family," presented Bunker as the quintessential bigot. His bigotry was so blatant, his prejudice so practiced, that Archie shocked us all. When we listened to his inanities we were supposed to laugh at him and brace ourselves for his next barrage. When he spat out belittling terms for Poles, blacks or Jews, or when he snapped out demeaning words about women, especially to his long-suffering wife Edith, his behavior was so atrocious that the viewer was both to laugh and to wince.

But Archie Bunker was to have been more than a joke. He was supposed to be a force for changing attitudes in American society. The program attempted to bring about change in viewers, change from the narrow attitudes that many Americans have of racial bigotry and of all demeaning approaches to women.

Getting the Joke

The trouble with satire, however, is the risk one runs that some people will miss the point. There have been times Christian magazines have used satire as a means to challenge certain attitudes. The editors of these magazines have found that their letters column will be cluttered in the next issue by remarks of outraged readers who did not realize that the article that angered them was supposed to be a joke. When the joke has to be explained it loses its humor; when satire is labeled it loses its punch.

The problem in the early years of "All in the Family" was that some viewers did not get the joke. They laughed *with* Archie Bunker and not *at* him. Archie's bigotry reinforced their own pettiness; the belittling attitudes they had toward women and minorities were strengthened not weakened. Archie became the lovable bigot.

We remember one friend who spoke to us with enthusiasm about the program when it first aired. He said it was hilarious to find a program on television on which blacks and feminists were no longer coddled but got what they deserved. For him the outrageous behavior of Archie was an encouragement for further bigotry. Archie Bunker was supposed to be a joke. But for some people the joke was lost in new hatreds.

Archie's Bible Club

There was one more thing about Archie Bunker. Whenever he was really pressed into a corner, he would invoke God and Bible on his side. Archie's god was a white Protestant, inner-city male deity with the same prejudices that Archie had; his bible was a blunt instrument to bash down all opposition to his attitudes. Archie used his god and bible as tools for last-ditch defense. God for Archie was not a person of wonder or an object of worship, nor was the Bible a book for devotion and instruction. Archie used God as a hammer and the Bible as a club.

Archie was designed to make us react. We were supposed to laugh at his god and his bible as we laughed at him. In this regard, "All in the Family" was a potent force for the secularizing of American culture.

Lemon Meringue Voices

For us, the most disquieting issue was Archie's use of God and Bible to defend his views. On one program, there was a discussion of the possibility of a network news anchor job going to a woman. Archie's retort was something like this: "God gave women voices to ask if you want lemon meringue pie, not to announce World War III." How, he asked, could a "lemon meringue" voice be taken seriously outside of taking orders at a restaurant?

Bunker's art of prejudice mirrored the nastiness of life. Pioneer anchorwoman Jessica Savitch was told early in her career that women's voices were not authoritative enough to broadcast tragedy. Network officials informed her that if a male reporter were to announce the midair crash of two 747s, the viewers would listen with attentive horror. If a woman were to announce the same thing, "the viewers would say, 'I don't believe it, not from a *woman.*'"[1]

It is no secret that women have had great difficulties in gaining serious recognition in the broadcast media. But the grating thing about Archie Bunker's put-down was his invocation of the person of God as designing women to have the wrong kind of voice to be taken seriously outside the context of food orders. The underlying philosophy was clear and infuriating: God's design for woman was wrapped up in domestic chores. How dare a woman take off her scullery maid's apron and enter the domain of men?

For a woman to aspire to the position of newsanchor is most unsettling to the Archie Bunker approach to life. Such a woman, it might be judged, has not learned the basic rules of feminine passivity. Such a woman simply has not learned the first and most basic lesson of being feminine: a lemon meringue voice goes with a lemon meringue mind. As Dale Carlson writes, explaining to teenagers the rules of growing up female:

> Like every other girl, you have a lot to learn. And some of the lessons aren't easy. The first and most basic lesson, is learning to be stupid. You may already have discovered this.
>
> Learning to be stupid is hard. It takes years of work on your part, and an exhausting amount of

effort on the part of society. All of it intended to make sure that when you grow up, you will know practically nothing. Or at least a lot less than boys.[2]

Bigotry and Piety

There are Archies in many bunkers of our living. Some of these Archies are sitting in the pews of evangelical churches and not a few stand behind the pulpits. These Archies are not joking at all when they use God and Bible to reinforce their own attitudes of narrowness and bigotry as the proper stance of faith and piety.

Recently the chancellor of a well-known fundamentalist Christian college adopted a pose that Archie would have liked. This gentleman spoke against a renewed interest in space exploration. He avers that space exploration is wrong because "there may be things in the heavens God doesn't want us to see."[3] It seems to us hard to believe that such a sentiment would be expressed without a smile. It is as though just as there are things in heaven that God does not want us to see, there are things on earth God does not want us to hear. Among them are women broadcasters. Let's keep men on the earth and women in the kitchen.

Culture Shock

Many times men are quite unaware of how hurtful their Bunker-type boorish remarks are to women. Take the example presented by Kari Malcolm.

Kari Torjesen Malcolm, a daughter of Norwegian missionaries to China, spent her teenage years as a prisoner of the Japanese during World War II. After the war, Malcolm was able to attend Wheaton College to prepare herself for missionary service. One might think that a young woman whose youth was spent in a struggle for survival would be unflappable. In fact, Malcolm was in for serious and unexpected culture shock in college:

Culture shock hit in my very first class—speech. By the second day of class, students began giving practice speeches. To my amazement one day a young war veteran got up and proclaimed that women were going to college with the primary motivation of looking for husbands!

After years of waiting in prison to study at this particular Christian college to prepare for Christian service, I was being told in a public speech that my sense of destiny as a handmaid of the Lord was just a front for husband-hunting. What crushed me most was that nobody else in the room was bothered by the speech. They thought it was a big joke, while to me it touched on deep issues involving my identity as a disciple of Jesus Christ.[4]

It was only years later when Malcolm read Betty Friedan's first book that she realized she had confronted the "feminine mystique" among her Christian classmates. We will see more about this notion in our next chapter.

If the feminine mystique was only beginning to bloom in the midforties when Kari Malcolm entered Wheaton College, why have the petals not finally fallen from this sorry bloom four decades later? This strange flower is still there; its unpleasant aroma may be detected in many places.

Item: At the seminary where Ron teaches, a male student looks at the young woman seated in the desk next to his on the first day of class and asks, "What are you doing here? Don't you know most of us are already married?"

Item: In a conference Beverly is attending, a woman speaks at the lunch table about the way her husband used to help with the children but does so no longer; she is not permitted any time out of the house away from the children because she, not he, is the mother.

Item: In a church where Ron is preaching, a woman who has had a rewarding business career has recently married in midlife; she asks if it is really true that a Christian wife who works outside the home for other than short-term, emergency reasons is shaming her husband before the Lord.

Item: In a book Beverly is reading she comes across a passage in which a man, speaking on behalf of biblical morality, decries the fact that women were given the vote in this country because that is a part of the humanist conspiracy to destroy the American family.[5]

Item: In the opening service of a missions conference, each of the men missionaries is given five minutes to present his opening remarks. A highly regarded veteran woman missionary is told that she may share some of her experiences at a ladies' tea, but is only to say her own name and the name of her field when she stands at the pulpit.

Item: In a radio talk show the following interchange is reported:

> Caller: "Why can't women preach and teach?"
> Minister: "That ministry is for men only and I can give you a very good reason: God made roosters to crow and hens to lay eggs."[6]

Item: In a local church in our community, several members of a home Bible study group objected that the discussion guide suggested for the group of mixed adults was written by a woman. The Minister of Christian Education salved the consciences of those who complained: "All the writer is doing is suggesting avenues for discussion; she is not really *teaching* you anything!"

Given these attitudes, even in the church, is it any wonder there is a women's movement in our day?

The Little Ladies, God Bless 'em!

But just mention the women's movement to the Archie Bunkers in the church, and you will find this brings out their best (or worst). When it comes to the roles of women and men, the Archie Bunkers of the church have their sway. These Archies are not joking; they are very serious indeed. When they pontificate their prejudices they are not looking for a laugh; they are seeking "Amens" from their corner (and perhaps funds for their campaigns).

One of the ways the contemporary women's movement is dismissed by opponents in the church is through the use of demeaning language such as "women's libbers" or "bra burners." By using such trivializing language, it is hoped the whole thing will go away and not bother us any more. The approach seems to be: Let's let the little ladies, God bless 'em, get this out of their system. Then things will return to normal.

Feminists and . . .

A more insidious approach is based on hatred and fear and finds expression in the racial prejudice of anti-Semitism. Some of the prominent women in the secular movement for women's rights are people of Jewish background. This factor has caused some who are against the women's movement to dismiss the entire quest for women's dignity as "a Jewish plot." For several years now, Ron has been involved in ongoing discussions with Jewish leaders of our community as part of an evangelical-Jewish dialogue. These discussions have raised our consciousness concerning the intractable forces of anti-Semitism in Western culture. We tend to think of anti-Semitism as something of the past. The moment we relax, however, it springs up again. It is particularly grievous to find Christian people attacking ideas they do not like by using the labels and tactics of hatred instead of reason, of fear instead of love.

Guilt by association is another tactic used by those who wish to avoid the real issues of injustice many women feel in today's world. This is a common method used by a debater whose more principled approaches are not working well. Some provocateurs like to form a link in the Christian mindset between women's quest for dignity and a long litany of evils, thus sullying the entire women's movement.

The Company You Keep

This tactic has been used by various hate groups for years. Our family experienced the blunt end of this ploy one summer nearly twenty years ago when we came under serious personal threat by the Ku Klux Klan. A rumor had spread throughout the little southern town where we were living that Ron's activities in selling Bibles door-to-door was in fact a front for inciting black field workers to strike against the tobacco growers during the harvest. This was a time of great racial unrest; Martin Luther King, Jr., was believed to be coming to this county to direct the strike, and we, the newcomers with our foreign way of talking, were judged to be his organizers. We had a difficult time quelling the lies about us, and we lived under some fear: at one point a church deacon of a fundamental, Bible-believing church and a secret member of the Klan, pointed a rifle at Ron and threatened the life of our baby daughter Laureen.

When we were finally cleared of these false charges and given police protection, we sought the reasons for all the nastiness against us. A Klan insider gave us the explanation: white outsiders who were religionists were tied together in the same knot with "blacks, perverts, and commies." For just a moment of our lives our family experienced the edge of the shadow of the darkness of racial prejudice. We have no understanding of what it might be like to experience a lifetime of hatred.

As the Klan links "blacks, perverts, and commies" in their litany of evils, so the conservative opponents of the women's movement recite their own list of the evils of feminism. They then dismiss the whole issue as a satanic plot. It is a common practice to equate the pursuit of dignity for women with the following:

- a necessary breakdown of family values
- the strident advocacy of gay rights
- a forthright championing of abortion.

Hate one, hate them all. Here is a domino theory of social change.

Now, we must not gloss over facts here. Many who are involved in the women's movement *have* promoted these very things. Many have broken from their families, do advocate gay rights, and do insist on abortion on demand as "the mother's right to choose," or "reproductive freedom" (one of the most ghastly euphemisms outside an Orwell novel of the destruction of life). It is not difficult at all to document each of these issues in the writings of the leading feminists (and we do so in the next chapter).

A Litany of Evils

One group of women that opposes the activism of feminists in the United States recently sent out a fund raising letter that charges the contemporary women's movement with the advocacy of numerous immoralities that would upset any "God-fearing, pro-moral Christian woman." Here is an extract from their letter.

Here are some of [feminism's] goals:

- They have adopted a lesbian rights resolution with a goal to make lesbianism and homosexuality an acceptable lifestyle.
- They have adopted a reproductive rights resolution which favors the continuance of abortion on demand.
- This resolution also contains a battle plan to defeat any and all anti-abortion groups and legislation based on the "right-to-life" of the unborn.
- They have adopted a school prayer resolution, opposing voluntary prayer in the classroom.
- They have adopted a resolution opposing tuition tax credits for private schools.
- They have adopted a nuclear weapons resolution demanding the United States Government freeze all research development, testing, production, deployment, exporting and recycling of nuclear weapons and their tactical support systems.[7]

We have some observations to make here. The first concerns this listing of the perceived evils of feminism; the items simply are not of the same level. We judge the issues of the advocacy of abortion on demand and the promotion of a homosexual life-style to be blatantly unbiblical and truly abhorrent to most evangelical Christian women and men. We conclude that these evils are rightly to be opposed.

But "pro-moral Christian women"—and men—(are there antimoral Christian women?) have considerable room for disagreement on the issues of prayer in the school room and the concept of tuition tax credits. These are hardly moral issues of the same order as the others, and genuine Christian believers may come down on either side on these points. We confuse people by linking issues of dissimilar weightiness and uneven agreement among Christians by suggesting there is only one truly Christian point of view on them.

Moreover, it is a slur on many deeply Christian women to judge the concept of a nuclear freeze to be obviously immoral. It is a point of fact that leading evangelical governmental leaders as well as lay people line up on both sides of the debate of how best to avert a nuclear holocaust.

Our second observation is that there is a tendency on the part of some opponents to regard these several issues as necessary links in the same chain; some believe this is a chain forged in the pit. Hence, the argument goes, all feminist concerns should be dismissed. Instead of stating strong opposition to certain issues, ambivalence about others, and even acceptance of some, there is a wholesale rejection of all issues that come from feminism.

The Daughters of Light and Darkness

Further, we are concerned about the militaristic and apocalyptic tenor that marks some traditionalist, antifeminist rhetoric. The language is not unlike what we find in the Qumran (Dead Sea Scroll) document, *The War of the Sons of Light Against the Sons of Darkness*. In that text there is a use of strident language that is frightening. In some of the traditionalist pamphleteering there is a call to arms that sounds like the final battle is approaching:

> The women of this nation are at a crossroads of history. The battle lines are becoming more clearly defined. The forces of Darkness are becoming darker. There is no neutral ground in the battle to come.[8]

In balance, however, we wish to join the sentiment of Concerned Women for America in rejecting the arrogance of such feminist groups as the National Organization for Women (NOW) in their presumptuous claims that they speak for the women of America. If for no other reason than to cry foul against an unfair tactic, traditionalists such as Beverly LaHaye, the president of Concerned Women for America and the wife of Moral Majority cofounder Tim LaHaye, and Phyllis Schlafly, the president of Eagle Forum and an outspoken foe of the women's movement, should be applauded. Millions of women (and men) are neither sympathetic to nor supportive of the goals of the secular feminist movement.

We are also appalled at the often unfair and unfounded tactics employed by leading secular feminists in their sustained attacks on traditional forces working for public morality. For example, in a recent article, Gloria Steinem, long associated with *Ms.* magazine, is quoted (approvingly) as advocating many forms of sexual license. She then gives her clincher: "No longer will sex be seen as only a way of having children, which is the stand taken by the Moral Majority."[9] This is a blatant distortion of the well-known positions of the Moral Majority. This group has spoken strongly against overt homosexuality and abortion on demand, but never has taken a stand that "sex is only a way of having children." Steinem is here guilty of deliberate distortion of an opponent's point of view in an attempt to make her own position sound reasonable. Most readers, we fear, will not realize her deception, and will just chuckle away at those Moral Majority folks.

There is overstatement on both sides. In some evangelical circles the term *feminism* is perceived to be *the* evil of our age, a scapegoat to be driven into the wilderness. In some feminist circles, male evangelical Christians are painted as red-neck women haters and their women as traitors to their sex.

Coupled to overstatement is the fact that no one seems to be listening to the other, except to find an outrageous quotation to use in furthering the debate.

Feminism is a hardball issue today. Move over, Mother Goose! It turns out that in addition to sugar and spice and all things nice, little girls—and their mothers—are made of not a little grit and considerable tempered steel. One thing is sure: there is no longer any room for the Archie Bunker one-liners. No one is laughing any longer.

We are all in too much turmoil for that.

Chapter 1, Notes

1. Michael Mallowe, "Jessica Savitch Reconsidered," *Savvy: The Magazine for Executive Women*, September 1984, 61. Savitch died at the age of thirty-five as the car driven by her companion Martin Fischbein plunged into the Delaware Canal near New Hope, Pennsylvania, on 24 October 1983. Earlier that day the couple had attended church services at the Marble Collegiate Church in New York and had heard famed pastor Norman Vincent Peale. Savitch's disappointing autobiography, *Anchorwoman* seemed to gloss over much of her troubled life (New York: G. P. Putnam's Sons, 1982). Gloria Steinem speaks on the difficulties women have had in entering the broadcast news media: "Female reporters were kept out of television and radio for years by the argument that their voices were too high, grating, or non-authoritative to speak the news credibly. Even now, women's voices may be thought more suitable for human interest and 'soft news,' while men still announce 'hard news.' In the early days of television, women were allowed to do the weather reports—very sexily." *Outrageous Acts and Everyday Rebellions* (New York: New American Library, 1984), 187. Archie Bunker's observations about "lemon-meringue" voices should include "partly-cloudy-with-some-clearing" voices as well.

2. Dale Carlson, *Girls Are Equal Too: The Women's Movement for Teenagers* (Forge Village, Mass.: Atheneum, 1973), vii. Other essential lessons that Carlson says society presents to girls include: learning to be inferior, how to be passive, learning dependency, and being adorable. Most of all, the girl is to be NICE about it.

3. *USA Today*, 9 August 1984.

4. Kari Torjesen Malcolm, *Women at the Crossroads: A Path Beyond Feminism and Traditionalism* (Downers Grove, Ill.: InterVarsity Press, 1982), 24-25.

5. The speaker was Howard Phillips, National Director of the Conservative Caucus, speaking at a "Pro-Life Rally" on 12 July 1980 in Long Beach, California, under the auspices of Citizens for Biblical Morality, an arm of Moral Majority. This story is reported by Anne Bowen Follis in her book, *"I'm Not a Woman's Libber, But . . ." And Other Confessions of a Christian Feminist* (Nashville: Abingdon, 1981), 56-57.

6. "Point of View," afternoon call-in program on WBRI, Indianapolis (21 March 1967), cited by Letha Scanzoni and Nancy Hardesty, *All We're Meant to Be: A Biblical Approach to Women's Liberation* (Waco, Tex.: Word Books, 1974), 169. On the same page, Scanzoni and Hardesty point out the time Archie Bunker ended a theological debate with his wife: "Stifle yourself, Edith. God don't want to be defended by no dingbat!"

7. Undated fund raising letter (received 16 October 1984) from Beverly LaHaye on behalf of Concerned Women for America (CWA, a countergroup to NOW, the National Organization for Women). The formation of CWA was noted in a newsarticle in *USA Today*, 30 September 1983, and in an interview article in *Fundamentalist Journal*, April 1984, 41-43.

8. Beverly LaHaye, *Who But a Woman?* (Nashville: Thomas Nelson, 1984), 13.

9. Betsy Carter, "Liberation's Next Wave, According to Gloria Steinem," *Esquire*, June 1984, 205.

Who knows what women can be when they are finally free to become themselves? Who knows what women's intelligence will contribute when it can be nourished without denying love? Who knows of the possibilities of love when men and women share not only children, home and garden, not only the fulfillment of their biological roles, but the responsibilities and passions of the work that creates the human future and the full human knowledge of who they are? It has barely begun, the search of women for themselves. But the time is at hand when the voices of the feminine mystique can no longer drown out the inner voice that is driving women on to become complete.

Betty Friedan
The Feminine Mystique

Chapter 2

The Movement and the Mystique

W ho we are as male and female has become one of the most difficult questions of our day. This does not seem to be an item that will flitter away as new concerns come to us. Rather, the concept of male and female issues keeps pressing in upon us with more urgency than ever and leaves us with new questions. We must confront the issue of feminism head on; it is indeed a critical concern.

Feminism—An Odious Term?

It is understandable, however, that many evangelicals are chary even to discuss the word feminism. The perceptions of feminism are so negative as to leave a discussion of the issues beyond the pale. Better a discussion of the salvation of frogs. For those evangelical writers who have presented biblical critiques of feminism, usually the focus is strictly upon feminist treatments that claim to be based on the Scripture and which proceed from an evangelical Christian faith. Susan Foh, for example, has written a thoughtful and articulate response to the biblical arguments for feminism found in the writings of Letha Scanzoni and Nancy Hardesty, Virginia R. Mollenkott and Paul

K. Jewett. Foh's book is an able presentation and development of biblical traditionalism,[1] but it is a presentation of the arguments of one set of evangelical Christians against the arguments of another set of evangelical Christians. That is, her book argues against the issue of feminism within a very limited compass. We believe it is time for evangelicals to deal with feminism from the vantage point of the movement as a whole, and not just that of varying factions within our circles of faith, friendship—and disputation.

Diversity

What is the women's movement? We wish to suggest that the evangelical does not have to write off feminism altogether because of some of the odious causes (such as divorce, abortion, and lesbianism) that many feminists espouse.[2] For there are issues in addition to the dissolution of the family, the destruction of the unwanted unborn, and the advocacy of homosexuality as a socially-approved alternative that the women's movement rightly raises, and that concern Christians as well as non-Christians.

At its base, the modern women's movement is an attempt on the part of many women (and men) to assert for women *genuine dignity and worth as persons* and to break through what they believe to be the many oppressive barriers with which traditional culture binds them. A potent phrase of the goal of feminists is the realization of a sense of *full, authentic personhood*.

As in any social movement of moment, there are significant divergences of opinion as to what feminism is or ought to be. We would be as mistaken if we approach feminism as a monolithic block as Christians are in speaking of "the Jews," (or Jews are in speaking of "the Christians"). Some feminists are content only to argue that women are people too (a phrase associated with Alan Alda). Dorothy L. Sayers, famed author of the Lord Peter Wimsey mystery series (also a learned medievalist), titled her modest proposal, *Are Women Human?*[3]

For others, the women's movement will not be satisfied until there is general societal capitulation to the concept of full inter-changeability among the sexes in all areas except the obviously biological.

Radicalism

The most extreme feminists do not even draw the line on biological issues. (Gentle readers should be seated here.) Shulamith Firestone is representative of this most radical posi-tion. She longs for a day in a socialist paradise where artificial insemination in test tube glasses and mechanical gestation of babies in the lab would replace the necessity for a woman to be identified with the womb.[4] Only when women no longer have to be associated with babies will women truly be free. Firestone believes that the fundamental flaw in Russian communism in es-tablishing the utopia envisioned by Marx and Engels was the failure of the Russian revolutionaries to eliminate the family and sexual repression.[5]

Firestone's feminist-Marxist view of the Messianic Age is a time when the biological family is completely destroyed and all restraints against deviant sexual expression have dissolved. We suspect that many Christians and conservative Americans who believe that the feminist movement is out to destroy the family may not quite realize how serious the matter really is in the constructions of a writer such as Firestone. Somehow the word *atheism* seems too mild a term to describe such a posi-tion.[6]

No Monolith

So there we have it. Feminism is not monolithic at all. There is abundant variety within the ranks of feminists, from those who only wish to assert that women are also people to those who wish to deny that there is any reality to the concept of the feminine. There is such diversity that some have suggested we speak not of the women's movement, but women's move-ments.

Most feminists are in the middle, not at the extremes. Most feminists are as appalled with Firestone as are traditionalists. Ten years later, mainstream feminists term Firestone and others like her an aberration. We need to know about radical feminism and seek to appraise its level of support. We must be aware of the radical extreme, just to know what we are up against in the worst possible scenarios. *But it is as unfair for evangelical Christians to describe feminism in terms of its most repugnant representations as it is for feminists to debunk evangelical Christians by citing our most outlandish pseudo-spokespersons as representing the whole.*[7]

The feminist movement is a revolution. As such it should be compared to other revolutions in Western tradition. Once a revolution is effected, the more moderate majority tends to suppress the radical extremists. The American revolution as well as the Protestant Reformation (yes, even the Russian revolution) are examples of this tendency. Although the radical revolutionary Thomas Paine served the American revolution, he died in ignominy; the moderate revolutionary George Washington is the nation's hero. The Protestant Reformation is defined by Martin Luther and John Calvin, not the radicals who smashed churches. Puritanism in early American history cannot be explained merely by the Salem witch trials. Again, an aberration should not be used for primary definition. The function of the "lunatic fringe" of any movement is only to show the outer limits of that movement.

Therefore, to understand feminism rightly, we need to look at the trunk and major branches; the twigs do not define the tree.

Definition

A serviceable definition of feminism is advanced by Denise Lardner Carmody: "By *feminism* I mean the advocacy of women's equality with men, sensitivity to the injustices women have suffered, and the resolution that women come into their own without delay."[8] Equality, injustice, and action. These, not deviant sexual practices, are the principal issues.

Where It Began

The catalyst for the modern women's movement in the United States was the publication of Betty Friedan's *The Feminine Mystique* in 1963. (We mentioned her book in the previous chapter as we described the experience of Kari Malcolm at Wheaton College in the midforties.) It is difficult to overestimate the influence of this book on the direction of society in America over the last two decades. What Darwin's, *The Origin of the Species* is to evolutionary biology, and Wellhausen's, *Prolegomena to the History of Israel* is to recent biblical criticism, *The Feminine Mystique* is to women's liberation. This book was the spark that ignited the blaze of a modern movement of staggering proportions.

De Beauvoir

If Friedan ushered in the new messianic age of feminism, her "Jeanne the Baptist" was the pioneer French feminist, Simone de Beauvoir. De Beauvoir's two-volume work, *Le Deuzième Sexe*, was published in France in 1949. The English translation *The Second Sex* (first published in 1952) was the voice in the wilderness for the women's movement. Here are de Beauvoir's opening words, her salvo for women's liberation:

> Woman? Very simple, say the fanciers of simple formulas: she is a womb, an ovary; she is a female—this word is sufficient to define her. In the mouth of a man the epithet *female* has the sound of an insult, yet he is not ashamed of his animal nature; on the contrary, he is proud if someone says of him: "He is a male!" The term "female" is derogatory not because it emphasizes woman's animality, but because it imprisons her in her sex; and if this sex seems to man to be contemptible and inimical even in harmless dumb animals, it is evidently because of the uneasy hostility stirred up in him by woman.[9]

It was de Beauvoir's thesis that women have been made to occupy a second place to men from the earliest patriarchal period; though presumably constituting half of the population, women are the true minority in culture. De Beauvoir further argued that this secondary position was not based on intrinsic characteristics of femininity, but by the purposeful control of women by men through manipulative acts in culture and tradition.

De Beauvoir believes,

> One is not born, but rather becomes, a woman. No biological, psychological, or economic fate determines the figure that the human female presents in society; it is civilization as a whole that produces this creature, intermediate between male and eunuch, which is described as feminine.[10]

A Flood of Change

The last two decades have witnessed a frenzy of activity and a flood of change in American culture respecting women. A recent editorial in a men's magazine speaks of the rapidity of change and the questions that result for all of us:

> Some twenty years ago a slow-moving cultural shift in our society suddenly swelled into a flood of change, and the American woman underwent a process of redefinition that has few parallels. Even before the change took place, there had not been much question that the woman of the 1980s was going to be different from her 1960s counterpart. Changes in income levels, work patterns, sexual attitudes, and educational trends from the beginning of World War II to the 1960s all indicated that a major cultural shift was occurring. But no one could have foreseen how suddenly this movement toward women's total participation in society would take hold of the population and overnight become a force to be reckoned with. Not only would the redefinition of *woman* change society's mores and institutions, but it would provide women with an opportunity—an urgent mandate, even—to change the way they viewed *themselves.*[11]

Betty Friedan

This flood of change, as we have already noted, came largely in response to the forces set in motion two decades ago by the secular prophetess of feminism, Betty Friedan, and the publication of *The Feminine Mystique*. We recognize that for many evangelicals the mention of the name Betty Friedan raises countless red flags and sets off innumerable silent alarms. We also suspect that many such people have not read or interacted with the issues that Friedan presents. (Before we began our book, neither had we!) Now we have not only read her books, but have gone to hear her speak and have interacted with her ideas in several feminist group discussions.

We found Friedan's somewhat rambling oral presentation of her role in American feminism to be fascinating. She can be a warm and witty woman; she is certainly a convictionalist and a powerful communicator. Her ire was evidenced strongly against two groups of people—she is scathing in her contempt for those who oppose her from both the right and the left. When she was asked to evaluate traditionalist leader Phyllis Schlafly, Friedan snorted, "She is a disgrace and a traitor to her sex!" She was equally harsh on the type of men-haters and antifamily extremes of feminism that we have already noted: "This is not what we are; they are an aberration! They are not part of us!"[12]

We wish to present a brief survey of Friedan's principal ideas as a necessary backdrop for the argumentation of the rest of our book. As Kari Torjesen Malcolm suggests, let's at least listen to Betty Friedan as one might listen to a weather forecaster speak on the weather, even if we might not know about—or trust—that weather forecaster's views on God.[13]

The Journey Begins

Friedan described her personal journey, beginning with her growing up as a secular Jew in Peoria, Illinois, her career as a newspaper reporter which ended when she was fired for becoming pregnant with her second child, and her discovery of the limitations in the role of wife and mother in the midfifties in America. She stressed repeatedly how much things have changed in the last decades.

An indicative remark was the following: "For a woman to say, 'I am a person,' was a nearly revolutionary thing. You young women growing up today don't know what it was like to live within that tight girdle!" This is more than a laugh line; it is symptomatic.

Recently on vacation, the two of us were puzzled when we saw small couches displayed on the second floor landings of restored Victorian homes in Jacksonville, a small town in southern Oregon. We asked our guide why these couches were always placed in the hall at the head of the stairs. She explained that the greatly restraining corsets worn by women in the early years of this century so restricted their breathing that merely to climb a flight of stairs would cause them to swoon. These were even more confining than the girdles of Friedan's day. Who of us can even imagine what it was to have been a woman with bound feet in Old China?

Friedan studied women in American culture for a period of five years. Her study began with a survey of classmates who had graduated with her from Smith College in 1942. She found that in the fifteen years that had passed since their graduation, these women were facing a problem that was wrenching their lives apart, but it was a problem for which they had no name. Her studies extended to prolonged library research in sociology and psychology, extensive surveys of what was written for and by women in the popular magazines of the fifties, and intensive interviews of many women.

The Problem with No Name

Friedan found a level of desperation in the lives of many women in America that could not be dismissed. As she put it years later,

> We didn't admit it to each other if we felt there should be more in life than peanut-butter sandwiches with the kids, if throwing powder into the washing machine didn't make us relive our wedding night, if getting the socks or shirts pure white was not exactly

a peak experience, even if we did feel guilty about the tattletale gray.[14]

The inanities of Madison avenue in hawking new products were not bringing fulfillment to these women as persons. Women now had enviable tools for relieving the drudgery of housework, but housework, though it met few needs, still expanded in a Parkinson-manner to fill the available time. (And, as every reader of Erma Bombeck now knows, housework, if you do it right, will kill you!)

Friedan found that when women were finally able to articulate the "problem with no name," it was a desire for *more* than being wife and mother and homemaker. Women who had graduated from colleges in the early forties were finding it more and more stressful to feel any sense of well-being as housewives in the fifties. Although these women seemed to have achieved the American dream, they were keeping therapists occupied with expressions of their dissatisfaction. Friedan put it this way:

> If I am right, the problem that has no name stirring in the minds of so many American women today is not a matter of loss of femininity or too much education, or the demands of domesticity. It is far more important than anyone recognizes. It is the key to these other new and old problems which have been torturing women and their husbands and children, and puzzling their doctors and educators for years. It may well be the key to our future as a nation and a culture. We can no longer ignore that voice within women that says: "I want something more than my husband and my children and my home."[15]

The Feminine Mystique

Friedan termed the pervasive attitude of the late fifties—the attitude that glorified home and family as the real meaning for a woman—"the feminine mystique." Popular women's magazines of the time were speaking against the masculinizing of those women who had joined the work force in the decades before World War II. Being a a wife and a mother was glorified. A woman was not to think of herself as "just a housewife, but to be the master of many trades," an enviable position from which a woman should not wish to stoop. Fulfillment as a woman had only one definition—the housewife-mother. What a difference from the secular women's magazines of the eighties!

This then is "the feminine mystique" Friedan speaks against. This is a new, post-World War II restatement of the traditional view concerning women that Friedan believes has brought about such despondency among so many women. It was this influence that had sent women back to the home after the need for women in war-related industry had subsided. World War II was the great divide. During the war it was a matter of national survival for women to work outside the home; after the war it was a matter of national purpose for the working woman to return to the kitchen. Dorothy Sayers put it this way: "We will use women's work in wartime (though we will pay less for it), and take it away from them when the war is over."[16]

The feminine mystique is women finding fulfillment only in the home and family. It is the limitation of women to what the defeated Nazis had called *Kinder, Küche, Kirche*—concerns for children, cooking, and church.[17]

The feminine mystique was also an answer to what Friedan terms "the sexual solipsism of Sigmund Freud." This was Freud's scandalous view that women suffer from penis envy which they are only able to over come as they bear a male child whose penis is a substitute for their own deficiency.[18] Freud's studies of women, marked as much by his own conceptions as well as by the troubled lives of the Victorian women he interviewed, led him to believe that women are inherently deficient compared to men and that their wish to be equal with men is a mark of their common neurosis. Freud's views of women, though shocking to many readers today, had a profound effect on women in this country, especially in the forties.

The feminine mystique, Betty Friedan discovered,

> says that the highest value and the only commit-
> ment for women is the fulfillment of their own femi-
> ninity. . . . The mistake, says the mystique, the root
> of women's troubles in the past is that women envied
> men, women tried to be like men, instead of accept-
> ing their own nature, which can find fulfillment only
> in sexual passivity, male domination, and nurturing
> maternal love.[19]

The Sex-Role Revolution

For Friedan, and for the millions of women and men who
have been influenced by her writings, there needs to be an aban-
donment of the feminine mystique, for it is "burying millions of
American women alive."[20] Women have the same personal
needs for identity, for dignity, for personhood as do men. It is
not necessary to renounce femininity, to burn bras, and to hate
men to be free. But it is necessary to find ways to express truly
creative work to know oneself as a person. This will take a new
life plan, a new commitment to integrate marriage and motherhood with a serious involvement in society.

Ultimately, what Friedan called for was a revolutionary
change in society, "a sex-role revolution for men and women
which will restructure all our institutions."[21]

The Second Stage

Twenty-two years have past since Betty Friedan wrote *The
Feminine Mystique*. There are now young women and men who
have grown up with the ideals of feminism and the "holy quest"
for a sex-role revolution. These women have known only panty
hose, not confining corsets. But now new forces are at work.
Old line feminists are expressing fatigue. Many who marched
and fought for equity are now wondering where they are and
why they have come. Women who have sacrificed home and
family for career and fulfillment are wondering if the sacrifice

was worth the reward, if the gain was worth the cost.

These issues have so troubled Friedan that she recently has written a new book entitled *The Second Stage*. The first stage of the women's movement was to work for full participation for women within the mainstream of American life. While this quest for full participation presently is realized only in part, many things continue to trouble Friedan and other women:

> • Can the quest for personhood for women be achieved without the participation of men?
> • How shall women who are engaged in careers come to terms with the family?
> • How shall the polarization between men and women be bridged in a new wholeness?
> • How much longer can women pursue the Super-woman image?
> • How shall women face the new backlash against feminism?

In short, there is a new mystique that feminists are having to face today, the *feminist* mystique. Friedan says,

> I write this book to help the daughters break through the mystique I myself helped to create—and put the right name to their new problems. They have to ask new questions, speak the unspeakable again, admit new, uncomfortable realities, and secret pains and surprising joys of their personal truth that are hard to put into words because they do not fit either the new or old images of women, or they fit them disconcertingly.[22]

Faith of Our Fathers—and Our Mothers

Finally, there is one more element that concerns Betty Friedan these days. This was a major emphasis in her presentation to the Jewish women's conference in Portland. The founder and first president of the National Organization for Women (NOW), the original convener of the National Women's Political

Caucus, the woman who conceived of her own work for women in purely secular terms—this woman is now beginning to make her way on the road of return to the Jewish faith of her ancestors.

In a moving account, Friedan told of one of the most exciting days of her life as a feminist. On 26 August 1970 fifty thousand women paraded in New York City in what was billed the Women's Strike for Equality. The date was significant: fifty years earlier women gained the right to vote in this country.

As Friedan spoke to that largely secular group, she found herself strangely drawn back to the faith of her ancestors. She began to wonder if her passion against injustice was not more a part of her Jewish consciousness, which had been suppressed for so long. In that secular-yet-so-spiritual moment, she thought anew of the prayer in Judaism that is cited so often as an example of the patriarchy of that faith—the morning prayer of Jewish men:

> Blessed art Thou, oh Lord our God, King of the Universe, that I was not born a gentile.
> Blessed art Thou, oh Lord our God, King of the Universe, that I was not born a slave.
> Blessed art Thou, oh Lord our God, King of the Universe, that I was not born a woman.

Friedan recalled how she thought on that historic day, would it not be wonderful if on some day women of faith would be able to turn that prayer inside out and affirm their feminism in the context of covenant:

> Blessed art Thou, oh Lord our God, King of the Universe, *that I was born a woman*!

It is not a little thing for the secular Jewish woman who began the contemporary women's movement to speak—even obliquely—of her return to faith in God. For women and men of faith, feminism must be evaluated in the context of faith in God.

In the next chapter we will see how difficult this task has been. But at the end of this chapter, would it not be good for

each of us to affirm our own personal and sexual identity in a
creative, positive inversion of a traditionally sexist prayer?

> *I bless you, O my great God, King of the universe,*
> *and my Savior the Lord Jesus Christ,*
> *that you have made me who I am,*
> *and I bless you that you have made me a woman/man.*
> *Amen.*

Chapter 2, Notes

1. Susan T. Foh, *Women and the Word of God: A Response to Biblical
Feminism* (Grand Rapids: Baker Book House, 1980). A well-known text of
traditionalism still in wide circulation is Charles Caldwell Ryrie's, *The Role of
Women in the Church* (Chicago: Moody Press, 1958; original title: *The Place
of Women in the Church*); this book was written before the advent of the current
women's liberation movement.

2. Again, it would be foolish to attempt to deny the nearly universal support
for divorce, abortion, and lesbian "rights" among leading secular feminist
writers.

In fact, the situation in some areas is probably worse than some people fear.
Social critic Ellen Peck has written a disturbing (even sleazy) account of a
number of women who have embraced feminism, and has described their sad,
fragmented states. Some of the more outlandish women's groups in the early,
radical stages, called themselves WITCH (Women's International Terrorist
Conspiracy from Hell) and SCUM (the Society for Cutting Up Men)! One radical tract, *Toward a Female Liberation*, was particularly antagonistic toward
marriage, which it defined as "a relationship which is oppressive politically,
exhausting physically, stereotyped emotionally and sexually, and atrophying
intellectually. (A woman teams up with an individual groomed from birth to
rule, and she is equipped for revolt only with the foot-shuffling, head-
scratching gestures of 'feminine guile.')" Ellen Peck, *A Funny Thing Happened on the Way to Equality* (Englewood Cliffs, N.J.: Prentice-Hall, Inc.,
1975), 12, 98.

Simone de Beauvoir, for example, argued for abortion as a principal means
to free women "from slavery to reproduction," and lesbianism as a means
"whereby a woman who wishes to enjoy her femininity in feminine arms can
also know the pride of obeying no master" (*The Second Sex*, trans. by H. M.
Parshley [New York: The Modern Library, 1968], 121, 419). It can hardly be
coincidental that the frightful increase in abortions in the United States since
the *Wade v. Roe* decision of 1973, and the blatant and overt acting out of "gay
pride" beginning in the seventies, came during the strong rise and impetus of
the contemporay women's movement.

So we wish to be clear on this issue. Leading feminists *do* advocate abortion on demand as a central plank in their platform. Gloria Steinem, for example, describes her own awakening to feminism as a coming to grips with

abortion. She speaks of how she learned to admit to a secret abortion she had had as she heard other women giving personal testimony of their terrible experiences with illegal abortions in the late sixties (*Outrageous Acts and Everyday Rebellions* [New York: New American Library, 1983], 17-18). By 1980 Steinem came to the truly outrageous position that the anti-abortion lobby was Nazi in character! "If Hitler Were Alive, Whose Side Would He Be On?" (ibid., 305-26).

3. Dorothy L. Sayers, *Are Women Human?* Introduction by Mary McDermott Shideler (Grand Rapids: Wm. B. Eerdmans Publishing Co., 1971). Her address was given before a women's society in 1938—truly ahead of its time! A jacket blurb from a *New York Times* review says: "Miss Sayer's feminism is so forthright and commonsensical one wonders why the women's movement had to be more or less reinvented 30 years after she wrote essays like 'Are Women Human?'"

4. In our experience of reading feminist rhetoric, the audacity of Firestone is unsurpassed. Her attack on the biological family is sustained and frontal: "For the first time it is becoming possible to attack the family not only on moral grounds—in that it reinforces biologically-based sex class, promoting adult males, who are then divided further among themselves by race and class privilege, over females of all ages and male children—but also on functional grounds: it is no longer necessary or most effective as the basic social unit of reproduction and production. There is no longer a need for universal reproduction, even if the development of artificial reproduction does not soon place biological reproduction itself in question; cybernation [the automation of production by computers], by changing not only man's relation to work, but his need to work altogether, will eventually strip the division of labor at the root of the family of any remaining practical value" (Shulamith Firestone, *The Dialectic of Sex: The Case for Feminist Revolution* [New York: William Morrow, 1970], 250).

Marielouise Janssen-Jurreit says of Firestone: "No female theorist demanded the repeal of the biological division of labor or of natural reproduction of the species more compellingly than Shulamith Firestone. She regarded the abolition of pregnancy as an important element of feminist politics" (*Sexism: The Male Monopoly on History and Thought*, trans. by Verne Moberg [New York: Farrar, Strauss & Giroux, 1982], 155). Janssen-Jurreit's own proposal for sexual politics in the feminist revolution is for women to call a "birth strike": "Birth strike is the most important weapon in women's struggle, but it must be accompanied by a feminist mass strategy, because a declining birth rate also contains risks" (351). The twin risks are: (1) if not done by a sufficient number of women, the birth strike would lead to a two class system of birthing and nonbirthing women; (2) the loss of children would directly affect the jobs of many women in the service sector (school and health care, for example).

5. Firestone, *The Dialectic of Sex*, 240. W. Peter Blitchington describes the early attempts in communist Russia to follow the antifamily philosophy of Engels, and the disastrous results that followed. He says "the result of this experiment in 'liberation' was not a new family order but rather a frantic attempt to reestablish the old, traditional family" (*Sex Roles & the Christian Family* [Wheaton: Tyndale House Publishers, 1980], 31).

6. Firestone's concept of sexuality in her feminist "Messianic Age" (her term! ibid., 274), is that of "a more natural 'polymorphously perverse' sexuality" in which no relationship would be nonsexual—children with children,

children with adults, adults with adults—without any taboo whatsoever (272). A reading of Firestone drives us back with a new intensity to the words of Paul in Romans 1: "The wrath of God is being revealed from heaven against all the godlessness and wickedness of men who suppress the truth by their wickedness. . . . Therefore God gave them over in the sinful desires of their hearts to sexual impurity for the degrading of their bodies with one another. . . . Because of this, God gave them over to shameful lusts" (Romans 1:18, 24, 26). But even Paul did not know of a day when perversion would be called "naturally polymorphous," and would be advocated even between young children.

7. Consider the account of the tragic story of the followers of the Rev. Hobart E. Freeman's faith-healing sect in Noble County, Indiana. Freeman used to be a professor of Old Testament at an outstanding evangelical seminary and has a fine book on Old Testament prophets that is published by a highly reputable Christian publisher. But he deviated from his earlier theology and promoted the notion that true Christians should never use any medical services whatsoever, but are to rely completely on prayer for divine healing. David and Kathleen Bergmann, whom we presume to be loving parents and sincere Christians, withheld all medical care from their critically ill nine-month-old daughter, Allyson. When the little girl died of untreated meningitis as a result of parental neglect, Judge Roger Cosbey said in sentencing them to ten years in prison, "The preventable death of a child will not be tolerated by the law even when cloaked in the garments of religion" (Associated Press bulletin, *The [Portland] Oregonian*, 30 October 1984; a brief report was also in *US News & World Report*, 22 November 1984, 14). Our point is this: Evangelical views of divine healing cannot be based on the unconscionable teachings of a Hobart Freeman.

8. Denise Lardner Carmody, *Feminism & Christianity: A Two-Way Reflection* (Nashville: Abingdon, 1982), 21. Gloria Steinem, defines feminism as "the equality and full humanity of women and men" (*Outrageous Acts*, 3).

9. Simone de Beauvoir, *The Second Sex*, 3.

10. Ibid., 267.

11. Phillip Moffitt, "Friendship Between the Sexes," *Esquire*, June 1984, 12.

12. Through the kindness of some dear Jewish friends, the two of us were invited to attend a conference in Portland, Oregon, entitled, "The Emerging Jewish Woman" (28 October 1984). Betty Friedan's Keynote Address was titled, "The Emerging Jewish Woman: Identity and Community." Friedan's hostility toward Phyllis Schlafly was quick and sharp. Schlafly comes under repeated attack in radical feminist literature. Mary Daly, for example, speaks of her in this way: "As a sort of female Doctor Strangelove, Schlafly illustrates a consistency of pathology, combining machine-like callousness toward women with the same sort of indifference to all of Elemental nature and to all of life, except in fetal form" (*Pure Lust: Elemental Feminist Philosophy* [Boston: Beacon Press, 1984], 212. Perhaps Schlafly may take some solace, however; Daly is equally harsh on Mother Teresa, whom she describes as a woman-betraying masochistic model (ibid., 213, 214).

13. Kari Torjesen Malcolm, *Women at the Crossroads: A Path Beyond Feminism and Traditionalism* (Downers Grove, Ill.: InterVarsity Press, 1982), 25.

14. Betty Friedan, "Introduction to the Tenth Anniversary Edition," *The Feminine Mystique* (New York: Dell, 1974), 1.

15. Betty Friedan, *The Feminine Mystique*, 27. Friedan's experience was in a context of white, well-educated American women of the suburbs who wondered if there were not more for them in life than as wives and mothers. It was not until later that the women's movement expanded to a transracial and transclass movement. Gloria Steinem's early speaking tours were in concert with black feminists (particularly Florynce Kennedy), in a deliberate attempt to bring women of color into the movement (*Outrageous Acts*, 5, 355).

16. Sayers, *Are Women Human?* 45.

17. It is most distressing to read that neo-Nazis cherish the same ideals. Richard Butler, the leader of a neo-Nazi cult in the Northwest, the Church of Jesus Christ Christian Aryan Nations of Hayden, Idaho, proclaims: "the thoughts of Aryan woman are dominated by the desire to enter family life. Aryan woman brings true love and affection and a happy, well-run home to refresh and inspire her man. The world of contented womanhood is made of family: husband, children and home. It is a far greater love and service to be the mother of healthy Aryan children than to be a clever woman lawyer." (Tobby Hatley, "Aryan Nations: North Idaho's Neo-Nazis," *Northwest*, a Sunday supplement to *The [Portland] Oregonian*, 18 November 1984, 8.)

18. Friedan has a chapter in her book describing Freud's view of women and the influence this view has had in America since the forties, particularly among popular writers on women's issues. The conclusion of neo-Freudians was that " 'Normal' femininity is achieved, however, only insofar as the woman finally renounces all active goals of her own, all her own 'originality,' to identify and fulfill herself through the activities and goals of husband, or son," (*The Feminine Mystique*, 113).

Christian theologian Paul K. Jewett speaks of Freud's view of women and sexuality as "a crude bit of misogyny." (*Man as Male and Female: A Study in Sexual Relationships from a Theological Point of View* [Grand Rapids: Wm. B. Eerdmans Publishing Co., 1975], 152.)

Radical feminist Shulamith Firestone has a lengthy chapter on the role of Freudian theory in shaping inferior attitudes among women. She begins in these words, "If we had to name the one cultural current that most characterizes America in the twentieth century, it might be the work of Freud and the disciplines that grew out of it. . . . Freudianism has become, with its confessionals and penance, its proselytes and converts, with the millions spent on its upkeep, our modern Church" (*The Dialectic of Sex*, 46-47).

Marielouise Janssen-Jurreit also chronicles Freud's aberrant views of women ("There must be inequality, and the superiority of the man is the lesser evil") and his profound influence on the oppression of female sexuality in Western nations. She says, "For more than half a century, in the name of a liberating therapy, female patients were tormented by being forced to repress their clitoral sensation, to renounce their ostensible desires to be masculine" (*Sexism*, 239).

Letha Dawson Scanzoni aptly criticizes Freud's theory of penis envy: "One of the many helpful contributions of the contemporary women's movement, however, has been the insight that females are far less concerned about male penis deprivation than about male *privilege* deprivation." *Sexuality* (Philadelphia: The Westminster Press, 1984), 12.

19. Friedan, *The Feminine Mystique*, 37.

20. Ibid., 325.

21. Ibid., 370 ("Epilogue").

22. Betty Friedan, *The Second Stage* (New York: Summit Books, 1981), 18.

In earlier times the Kikuyu women held a superior position in society. They were cruel warriors, dominated the men, and practiced polyandry. Since women were terribly jealous, many men were condemned to death for adultery and minor offenses. Men felt they were treated unfairly and planned a revolt against women's absolute rule. The women, however, were physically stronger than the men and better warriors. So the men decided to rebel when the majority of women, especially their leaders, were pregnant. On a selected day the men seduced the female leaders and the majority of their followers. Within six months the women were practically immobilized as a result of pregnancy: men then took over the leadership of the society. They immediately prohibited polyandry and established polygamy.

Jomo Kenyatta
as cited by Marielouise Janssen-Jurreit in
Sexism: The Male Monopoly on History and Thought

Chapter 3

Feminism and Myths

*T*he Kikuyu people of Kenya are only one example of cultures with myths of an early matriarchy being superseded by patriarchy by means of stealth. It is unexpected in our technological age, but some women are seeking to reassert the ancient myths; they want the power back. Some of these women are outside the church and are contemptuous of faith; a few are within the church and are attempting to bring faith and myth together. In this chapter we will deal with some of these hard issues.

The crisis between feminism and the church comes to us in a number of ways. At times the challenge comes because of words or actions of subtle sexism in the name of religion; at other times it comes with the bold audacity of enraged women seeking entirely new patterns of relationships. The irritant that so troubles these women is the subtle sexism that surrounds us like Muzak in an elevator, but which we can no longer ignore as we have in the past; there is more to this problem than mere aural clutter. Unfortunately, some enraged women are looking for new myths to replace traditional values.

With Tights and Cape

It is a difficult thing for many men to accept, but there are women who are no longer willing just to ponder these things in their hearts. Some of these women have taken bold new offensives, and they startle the unwary.

In September 1972, Ron went to Los Angeles with several professors from the seminary to attend an International Congress of Learned Societies in the Field of Religion. Biblical scholars from all over North America and many countries of Europe and Asia crowded the grand ballroom of the Century Plaza Hotel. Several thousand scholars were about to hear an address by the world-renowned New Testament scholar Ernst Käsemann of the University of Tübingen.

Just before the lecture began there was a strange commotion to the right of the platform. Then something happened that stunned the audience. A small group of women rushed up to the platform and seized the microphone. The lead woman was dressed in blue tights and cape, her chest emblazoned with the "S" logo made famous in Superman comics. This "Superperson" and the women with her then announced, with a carnival barker's flourish, the program of seminars sponsored by the caucus of women professors of religion. Among the lectures were deliberately petulant titles such as "Phallic Worship: The Ultimate Idolatry." Somewhat understandably, the news reports the next day gave considerably more attention to the announcement of the women's caucus than to the featured lecture of the evening.

The point these women made was that theology may no longer be considered strictly a male preserve. The reactions of the largely male audience ranged from amusement ("Will you look at those girls!") to outrage ("What in the world are those women thinking?"). Most of us still did not realize how serious these women were.

Whose Path Is This?

The path that leads to the contemporary feminist religious caucus is long and tortuous. All along the way there have been questions about the role, rights, and responsibilities of women in the synagogue and in the church. Many of us are still quite confused concerning this road. We wonder if the road is right and if the signs are reliable; or is it possible the road is faulty and the signs are the deliberately misleading graffiti of the enemy?

Male Religion

Feminism is confronting the synagogue and the church today with a sustained assault and along several flanks. Some women express a mood of deep anger against the entire Judeo-Christian tradition, which is regarded as a principal cause for their distress. Simone de Beauvoir articulated this anger in these strong words in her critique, *The Second Sex*:

> Man enjoys the great advantage of having a God endorse the codes he writes; and since man exercises a sovereign authority over woman it is especially fortunate that this authority has been vested in him by the Supreme Being. For the Jews, Mohammedans, and Christians, among others, man is master by divine right; the fear of God, therefore, will repress any impulse toward revolt in the downtrodden female.[1]

These words of sarcasm express the rage that has led many women to reject conventional religion which they believe denies them a sense of worth and dignity. Activists are now seeking new myths to replace rejected realities.

The Mother Goddess

A new factor is now taking place within the women's movement to redress these ill effects, a bold return to the old paganism of the mother goddess cult of the ancient Near and Middle East. Interest in the goddess is so intense that some writers have coined a new term for the study of deity as goddess: *thealogy*.

Worship of the mother goddess was extensive in the early Near and Middle East. She was known by many names and was venerated over thousands of years in numerous cultures. Some

Christian readers know of the pervasive nature of the mother goddess cult in the ancient world through the anti-Roman Catholic tract, *The Two Babylons*, by Alexander Hislop. Hislop attempted to denigrate the veneration of the Blessed Mary by painting her with the same brush as the ancient mother goddess cult.[2]

It is difficult to believe, but the mother goddess has a new day with the rise of radical feminism. In their attempts to throw off what they believe to be male domination by means of a male deity, these women are looking for a new, female deity. They have found her in the oldest paganism of the ancient world.

When God Was Woman

Merlin Stone has developed a sustained attempt to promote a new appreciation in the modern world for the ancient worship of the mother goddess. In her book, *When God Was a Woman*, she argues that the earliest religion in the prehistoric Middle East was the worship of the goddess. She observes: "The archaeological artifacts suggest that in all the Neolithic and early Chalcolithic societies the Divine Ancestress, generally referred to by most writers as the Mother Goddess, was revered as the supreme deity."[3]

Stone's argument postulates that during the period of goddess worship, the status of women was high in all levels of society. Women were free to be leaders in government, religion, and commerce because their deity was a woman. Stone believes evidences of the worship of the mother goddess and the high status given to women in such a system may be found in many texts from the ancient Near East. She recounts the description that Diodorus gave of the worship of the goddess Isis in ancient Egypt:

> It is for these reasons, in fact, that it was ordained that the queen should have greater power and honour than the king and that among private persons the wife should enjoy authority over the husband, husbands

agreeing in their marriage contract that they will be obedient in all things to their wives.[4]

The Northern Invaders

The curse in Merlin Stone's feminist Eden-myth came in the form of northern invaders who brought with them from their homelands in the Caucasus (a region of modern Russia) the worship of a male deity. These Indo-Europeans, or Aryans, began moving into the Near and Middle East in prehistoric times, with written evidence of their waves of immigration beginning in the mid-third millennium B.C. They came with their battle axes, their feelings of racial superiority, their horse-drawn war chariots, and their male-dominance attitudes.

To India these men came and established the caste system and its attendant racism. To Iran these people came and brought a concept of the duality of light and dark as good and evil. They came to Sumer and Babylon and upset the worship of the goddess Inanna with new male gods Enki, Enlil, Anu, and Marduk. They came to Anatolia (modern Turkey) at about 2200 B.C. and became the ruling class of the Hittites with their horse-drawn war chariots and their iron weapons.

Aryan Jews?

The most astounding of Stone's claims is that the Levites of the Bible were not Hebrew (Semitic) at all, but were a subgroup of Indo-Europeans, known as the Luvians or Luwians who should be regarded as a distinct subgroup of the Hittites:

> Certainly the Hebrew people have never been thought of as Indo-European, and by the time they were settled in Canaan, after their stay in Egypt, the majority of them may have been Semitic. Yet there is one group that stands apart from the Hebrews and yet is counted as one of their tribes. These are the priestly Levites. This is surely the most controversial hypothesis yet suggested, but at the risk of

overwhelming religious, emotional and academic reactions, I suggest that the Levites may have in some way been related to the Indo-Europeans, most especially the Luwians, Luvians, Luwites, or Luvites as the various translations will have it.[5]

The Sham of Eve

The final step in Stone's audacious rewriting of ancient history is to suggest that it was the Aryan (!) Levites who foisted upon the Hebrews (and upon us their heirs) the myth of Eve in the garden as a desperate attempt to stamp out the worship of the mother goddess. By portraying Eve our mother as a silly girl who could so easily be duped by the serpent, and then as a sultry seductress who could so cruelly deceive Adam, reasons for trust and confidence in women would forever be undermined:

> The further I explored the rites and symbolism of those who revered the Divine Ancestress, the more convinced I became that the Adam and Eve myth, most certainly a tale with a point of view, and with a most biased proclamation for its ending, had actually been designed to be used in the continuous Levite battle to suppress the female religion.[6]

Stone believes the oppressive Levites, who hated the goddess religion, did everything in their power to destroy her worship and suppress the rights of women to insure that this religion would never rise again. This work of the Levites was done in the context of a surreptitious plot:

> The myth of Adam and Eve, in which male domination was explained and justified, informed women and men alike that male ownership and control of submissively obedient women was to be regarded as the divine and natural state of the human species.[7]

The loss of the rights of women, Stone argues, came with the loss of the *rites* of the mother goddess. While not advancing an argument necessarily to revive the ancient female religion in our day, she does believe that only as moderns realize the nature of the ancient conspiracy against women found in the pages of the Bible will people finally be able to break away from the influence of one of culture's greatest shams—the legend of Adam and Eve.

Why These Words?

It is possible for one to read these words, we suppose, and to think them so aberrant as not worth mentioning outside of a study of systematized delusion. Certainly it would not take a Ph.D. in ancient history for one to recognize the preposterous nature of the claim within Stone's tour de force that the Levites were quasi-Hittite Aryans!

Stone's book is replete with quotations from the Bible, a redundant proof of the principle that if one does not really care what the Bible teaches, it is possible to claim that it teaches whatever one desires. This principle is found in all sub-Christian cults and in many modern perversions of biblical faith. In this regard, Stone's book uses the Bible for a new, chic cause—feminism—just as John Allegro's *The Sacred Mushroom and the Cross* attempted to exploit the Bible for roots of what he pretended to be a sex and drug cult. (Allegro wrote his book in the midst of the sexual revolution and the drug culture of the sixties.)[8]

Some might wonder if there are people in our culture who might actually pick up on these ideas. Sadly, there is considerable enthusiasm in certain feminist circles for the concept of the mother goddess. There has even been a story on the religion page of our own local newspaper concerning a woman minister-witch who proclaims herself a priestess of paganism, a devotee of the mother goddess. Attendant to her paganism is a new interest in witches and the occult. Another radical feminist has gained national notoriety; she believes herself to be a modern witch and calls herself Starhawk.[9]

There are women who are so enraged at what they perceive

to be the evils against women in traditional Judaism and Christianity that ancient paganism, which is thought to glorify women, somehow begins to look attractive again.

These are some of the forces we face today when we attempt to think Christianly about women and men.

The Sin of the Church

Not all angry women are outside the church looking frantically for a religious substitute for the faith they have spurned. Other women are working from within the church seeking to make the church more open to the full equity of women. They are attracted to the goddess myth as well.

Denise Lardner Carmody, a Roman Catholic feminist scholar, presents an important example of the current direction of the feminist movement within liberal religious circles. Her desire is to speak both to nonreligious feminists as well as to nonfeminist Christians and to say that both may learn from and inform the other.

Carmody's rage against the traditionalism of the church vis-à-vis women knows little bounds. Consider these strident words:

> So the core of the feminist challenge to the received notions of Christian selfhood is that the Church's practice has sullied its high claims almost irreparably; for in its practice, both distant and recent, the Church has sinned against women egregiously. While saying that in Christ there is neither male nor female (Gal. 3:28), the Church has discriminated against women systematically. While making love the crux of Christian morality, the Church has come close to hating women, penalizing them for their sex, in no way loving female nature as well as male. While preaching that perfect love is supposed to cast out fear (I John 4:18), the Church's treatment of women has been so imperfect, so fear-riddled, that frequently it has been far worse than that

of secular society. Even today many churches grant women fewer rights in ecclesiastical law than secular societies grant women in civil law.[10]

Despite the anger expressed in this paragraph, it is Carmody's intention in her book to speak not only against the abuses against women within the church, but to appeal as well to those who are caught up in more radical feminism not to ignore or to reject religious faith altogether. It is her desire to strive for a sense of Concordia between "genuine feminists" and "genuine Christians."

Back to Mother

Evangelical readers of Carmody's book will have to brace themselves for her stridency and self-admitted spleen venting. Still, one must wonder what type of Christianity she projects when she suggests there is sufficient evidence "to make me consider the Buddha, Jesus, Muhammad, Confucius, and their like more kin than strangers," and finds "little difficulty being 'large-minded' about phenomena such as the reemergence of the Goddess." In fact, about the goddess she concludes: "Whether as a retrieval from prehistoric humanity, or as an imaginative play of the new witches, the Goddess can take a decent, defensible place in the pantheon, if we conceive 'divinity' with sufficient sophistication."[11]

"Sophistication" thus becomes a new word for paganism in the strange new world in which we live.

Carmody uses phrases such as "genuine Christianity" and "authentic Christianity" to describe her beliefs; she does not use "biblical Christianity" except to speak of the cartoon idiocy of traditionalists who quote the Scripture to back up their positions. Of these people she concludes with little charity: "such right-wing stupidity makes all of Christianity liable to contempt."[12]

Carmody's approach to Christianity is significantly removed from the received dogmas of the neighborhood catechism class. For her, "the Jesus story is both myth and history."[13] Her vantage point is the comparative study of world religions, not the creeds of the church. Her conception of Christ is so malleable she is able to write:

> Certainly one of the major tasks in the sophisti-
> cated reconception of divinity incumbent on Chris-
> tians for the world-religious future is to remove the
> Incarnation from pejorative mythology sufficiently
> to allow us to hold both the oneness of the Logos In-
> carnate and the valuable presences of God outside
> Christian symbolism (for example, in sincere God-
> dess religion).[14]

Perhaps it is on the basis of Carmody's confession of myth as a factor in Christian faith that she is able to speak of an open-ness to the myth of the divine goddess as not being out of line for needy women today:

> So, to achieve *her* proper golden mean, her love
> that radiates powerfully from a confident self to both
> God and neighbor, today's woman perhaps needs
> maternal rather than paternal imagery for God. This
> is the link to the Goddess that Carol Christ and other
> feminists have been making. When the ultimate
> power that runs the universe is symbolized in female
> terms, women gain a tremendous source of self-
> affirmation. If the Goddess is the way to express
> women's share in such ultimate power, Christian
> theology ought to open to the Goddess.[15]

The Worship of Calves

So, if we understand Carmody correctly, she wants in some way to hold on to the uniqueness of the (demythologized!) Incarnation of Jesus as the Logos of John 1, as well as accept such diverse manifestations of deity as in "sincere" (gasp!) god-dess religion. No wonder antagonists of feminism are so angry! We judge this syncretism to be the same sin as the outrage com-

mitted by Jeroboam I, the first king of the northern nation of Israel, following the death of Solomon in 931/930 B.C.

King Jeroboam began a practice of syncretism that finally
led to the complete destruction of the northern kingdom of Israel
in 722 B.C. What Jeroboam did was based on political realities.
He knew that if the people of his nation were to travel three times
a year to Jerusalem for the worship festivals of Yahweh, they
would have divided loyalties. Their hearts would never really
be free from the tug of Jerusalem, the capital of Judah. So
Jeroboam made golden images of the calf deities, which were
putative manifestations of Baal, and established them at Bethel
and Dan. He then said of them to a credulous people, " 'It is too
much for you to go up to Jerusalem. Here are your gods, O Israel, who brought you up out of Egypt' " (1 Kings 12:28).

By this act of political cunning (but spiritual sin!—
1 Kings 12:30), Jeroboam was able to hang on to the uniqueness
of the saving acts of Yahweh and to embrace the diverse manifestations of deity in "sincere" Baal worship.

Feminizing God

Not only does Carmody propose a synthesis of the God of
Scripture and the mother goddess of mythology as a step to
realizing the feminist kingdom of God on earth,[16] she is also ac-
tively involved in a process we might call the feminization of
God.

We will discuss later the issues raised by those who refuse
to speak of God only in patriarchal terms and advance the
"Father/Mother" language of the New Lectionary. Here
Carmody goes beyond an attempt to balance theological language and biblical imagery: in her approach God becomes the
divine feminine. This is seen in the feminine pronouns she uses
throughout her book. For example, in a splendid sentence that
has a deliberately provocative emphasis on the final reflexive
pronoun, she writes: "Freely, lovingly, with a self-moving deli-
cacy and largesse we shall never more than glimpse, God has
chosen to communicate *herself*.[17] In addition, she speaks of the

Holy Spirit in the feminine: "She serves as a second Paraclete, making that groaning prayer too deep for words where God prays to God, she frees us from all the men in funny hats, all the preachers with funny voices, who would co-opt our liberty."[18]

Christa

Carmody presents feminine language for the Father and the Spirit; an artist has completed the feminine trinity. Last Holy Week the final step was made in New York City where a crucifix representing Christ as a woman was displayed behind the altar at the (Episcopal) Cathedral of St. John the Divine. The 4-foot, 250-pound statue was sculpted by Edwina Sandys, a granddaughter of Winston Churchill. She termed the statue "Christa," a female Jesus Christ. The church's dean, the Reverend James Park Morton, greatly understated the case when he compared the female Christ to other cultural accommodations such as a black Christ or an Oriental Christ: "What hasn't been done visually is the female sexuality incarnate." Morton's superior, the Right Reverend Walter Dennis, Episcopal suffragan bishop of New York, was scandalized. The work of art to him was "theologically and historically indefensible."[19]

With the person of Jesus Christ pictured as a woman, it would seem the feminization of the Holy Trinity is accomplished. These are the dimensions of liberal religious feminism in our day.

Imaging God

Carmody's advice to the other sisters who share her vistas of the worship of God (or the goddess?), and who no longer wish to listen to the men in the funny hats and the preachers with the funny voices: "Go to a church that honors your imaging of God. If you can't find such a church, form your own."[20]

Her words are symptomatic: the liberal religious feminist does not desire to reflect the image of God in which she (or he) was created; rather these activists wish to make God in their own image. This is the end result of the new mythologies: God is projected, not reflected; God is made, not the Maker.

Needless to say, biblically informed Christians will not wish to follow the lead of secular feminists such as Merlin Stone, with her quest for the goddess, nor the path of liberal religious feminists such as Denise Carmody, with her vision of a Christianity so flexible it may expand to include the goddess notion. These may be roads of rage, but it is hardly possible to confuse these roads with the revealed path of faith in the God of Scripture. Only unrestrained anger could keep one from seeing how patently false these pathways truly are. But we need at least to be aware of these paths and be prepared to gauge their influence on our culture.

Our Path

But evangelical women (and men) are subject to the same provocations as are the more liberal religionists. Why should a woman in a seminary class in the eighties suffer the same assault on her personal dignity that Kari Malcolm faced in a college class in the forties? In a generation, one would think that evangelicals would be ready to move to the second stage of balance; in fact, many of us have not even entered the first stage of participation.

Nonetheless, evangelical women (and men) do not wish to form new myths or adopt old paganisms, making gods in our image. What we do wish to do is to learn how to understand genuine biblical realities as they relate to living as authentic men and women who reflect the image of the true God who has created us.

Chapter 3, Notes

1. Simone de Beauvoir, *The Second Sex*, trans. H. M. Parshley (New York: The Modern Library, 1968), 621. This quotation appears several times in feminist literature, both secular and Christian.

2. See Alexander Hislop, *The Two Babylons, Or: The Papal Worship Proved to Be the Worship of Nimrod and His Wife*, first published in 1916 (reprint of 2d ed.; Neptune, N.J.: Loizeaux Brothers, 1959). On page 21 Hislop speaks of "the great Goddess 'Mother.'" Dallas Theological Seminary Professor J. Dwight Pentecost has popularized some of Hislop's conclusions in his

books on biblical prophecy, respecting the spiritual aberrations prophesied in Revelation 17. See *Prophecy for Today* (Grand Rapids: Zondervan Publishing House, 1961), 125-38.

3. Merlin Stone, *When God Was a Woman* (San Diego: Harcourt Brace Jovanovich, 1978), 18. Throughout her book, this author uses capital letters for nouns and pronouns referring to the female deity and lower case for similar references to the (male) deity of Scripture. We have reversed the practice, speaking of the "mother goddess."

4. Ibid., 36. Diodorus' description of women in ancient Egypt is buttressed by Herodotus: "Women go in the market-place, transact affairs and occupy themselves with business, while the husbands stay home and weave." However, Stone does not go on to say that Diodorus, a contemporary of Julius Caesar, is not regarded as a reliable authority in the very early periods of ancient history he describes. It is characteristic of Stone to quote texts that fit her theory without evaluating their veracity.

5. Ibid., 104. The first line of this quotation is incredible: "Certainly the Hebrew people have never been thought of as Indo-European." Such a sentence is akin to saying, "Certainly rabbits have never been thought of as chimpanzees." Even a sympathetic reader of Stone's book would have room for pause at this absurdity. Yet she is unfazed. The implications of the concept of "Aryan Hebrews" as against the atrocities committed by the Nazi "Aryans" during the holocaust are not lost on Stone. In fact, she goes one better: she suggests that the word *Nazi* may ultimately be related to Hebrew *nasi* ("prince") and that "Hitler" means "teacher of Hit"—a link to the Hittites! (127). Such arguments boggle the mind.

6. Ibid., 198. Stone's conclusions are so thoroughly antibiblical that we find it amazing that a Presbyterian minister who has written a biblical case for feminism has based part of his work on her writings. See Philip Siddons, *Speaking Out for Women—A Biblical View* (Valley Forge, Pa.: Judson Press, 1980), 39-40; in a footnote respecting the issue of "Aryan Levites," he does add, "Many, however, may find proof lacking for this" (ibid., 97). Indeed!

Convenient and trustworthy accounts of the peoples of the ancient Near East can be found in D. J. Wiseman, ed., *Peoples of Old Testament Times* (Oxford: At the Clarendon Press, 1973). Edwin Yamauchi has worked long and hard for responsibility in the use of ancient sources. An example is his review article, "Meshech, Tubal, and Company," *Journal of the Evangelical Theological Society* 19:3 (Summer 1976): 239-47. See now his full presentation, *Foes from the Northern Frontier: Invading Hordes from the Russian Steppes* (Grand Rapids: Baker Book House, 1982).

7. Ibid., 218. The flagging of the story of Adam and Eve as a sexist tool to hold women down in an inferior status to men is standard fare in secular feminist literature. The German feminist Marielouise Janssen-Jurreit, for instance, writes: "The myth of the Fall and the expulsion from Paradise was an instrument of the absolute power of patriarchal Western civilization. It represented woman's permanent inferiority; without this myth the European witch trials, for example, are unimaginable" (*Sexism: The Male Monopoly on History and Thought*, trans. Verne Moberg [New York: Farrar, Straus & Giroux, 1982], 98). That which is distinct in Stone's approach is the claim that the story of Adam and Eve was a plot concocted by non-Semitic male overlords in ancient Jewish culture.

8. Another example is Erich Von Daniken's chic sham *Chariots of the Gods*, in which he argued that the great innovations in the ancient period came from extraterrestrial visitations, which the benighted Hebrews mistakenly labeled as theophanies of God. James W. Sire evaluated these abuses of Scripture in his *Scripture Twisting: 20 Ways the Cults Misread the Bible* (Downers Grove, Ill.: InterVarsity Press, 1980), 78-79.

9. See Starhawk (Miriam Simos), *The Spiral Dance* (San Francisco: Harper & Row, 1979).

10. Denise Lardner Carmody, *Feminism & Christianity: A Two-Way Reflection* (Nashville: Abingdon, 1982), 88-89. She notes specific feminist concerns against the church such as abortion, contraception, homosexuality, and divorce, then states: "With more than sufficient evidence, feminists have concluded that Christianity makes people crazy in sexual matters, especially men. So, most feminists have labeled Christianity a foe of their sexual self and vowed to oppose it implacably" (90).

Carmody is not dispassionate. She speaks of "this dazzling combination of ignorance and arrogance" on the part of one nonreligious feminist, and of "outbursts of idiocy equally offensive" that come from antifeminists within the religious right (17, 18). For radical lesbians and fundamentalist Christians, she has equal contempt (12). Her hope is for "the day when humanistic feminism and deep Christianity see how much they coincide" (19).

11. Ibid., 167.

12. Ibid., 18.

13. Ibid., 34.

14. Ibid., 169.

15. Ibid., 52. Carol P. Christ, to whom Carmody refers, has written "Why Women Need the Goddess," in *Womanspirit Rising*, eds. Carol P. Christ and Judith Plaskow (San Francisco: Harper & Row, 1979). Carol Christ believes that traditional Judaism and Christianity cannot give women the support they need as women because the religious symbols in these religions are exclusively male (*Womanspirit Rising*, 275). It is for these reasons that she argues that women need a goddess which they may find in part in themselves.

A quotation developed by Christ (ibid., 273) has become a favorite of liberal religious feminists: "I found God in myself and I loved her fiercely." These words come in a climactic chorus at the end of a feminist play by Ntosake Shange, *For Colored Girls Who Have Considered Suicide When the Rainbow Is Enuf.*

16. She speaks of the realization of eschatology in Christian experience, suggesting: "As some interpret Johannine theology, the end-time of these things is already here" (ibid., 171).

17. Ibid., 169. At another point she writes: "God is never really God if finite senses and intelligences can comprehend her" (ibid., 40).

18. Ibid., 170.

19. "'Christa' Statue Gets Praise, Hoots," Associated Press story by Nick Ludington, appeared in *The [Portland] Oregonian*, 25 April 1984.

20. Carmody, *Feminism & Christianity*, 171.

Women are not human. They lie when they say they have human needs; warm and decent clothing; comfort in the bus; interests directed immediately to God and His universe, not intermediately through any child of man. They are far above man to inspire him; they have feminine minds and feminine natures, but their mind is not one with their nature like the minds of men; they have no human mind and no human nature. "Blessed be God," says the Jew, "that hath not made me a woman."

Dorothy L. Sayers
Are Women Human?

Chapter 4

Feminism and Faith

*T*hey were five Hebrew sisters. Their names were Mahlah, Noah, Hoglah, Milcah, and Tirzah. These young women had no brothers and their father was deceased. They did an extraordinary thing, these five women. They came into the presence of Moses at the entrance of the tent of meeting, and they expressed their concern for fairness for themselves and justice for their father's memory.

The Patriarch Moses

What it must have been for these five sisters to have come to Moses! Moses had stood before Yahweh on Mount Sinai when the mountain convulsed and the hills danced. Moses had been criticized and mocked for a generation; his critics had been silenced by plague, scourged by leprosy, swallowed by the earth. Moses was the servant of Yahweh, the voice of God. Yet these daughters of Zelophehad came before him at the sacral meeting place of God and man. There they faced Moses and those with him, Eleazar the high priest and the noble male leaders of each of the twelve tribes, and they said:

"Our father died in the desert. He was not among
Korah's followers, who banded together against the
LORD, but he died for his own sin and left no sons.
Why should our father's name disappear from his
clan because he had no son? Give us property among
our father's relatives" (Numbers 27:3-4).

The people of Israel were on the lip of the land of Canaan.
Only a river lay between them and Jericho, the first fruits of the
land. The wilderness was behind them and the land of promise
before them. The men of each tribe had been numbered for war
as their fathers had been numbered nearly forty years earlier.
Each family, each father's house was longing for the gift of a
parcel of land after living in a world of sand.

What About Women?

But the land would go only to men, only to a father's
household. It would be kept within the family as a perpetual possession. Provisions had already been made so that even the land
that might be imperiled for a time would ultimately revert to the
family line that had first held it.

The fathers and mothers of these people had been slaves in
Egypt. The new generation had grown to adulthood in the wilderness. But just over the Jordan lay the prospective family
homesteads that were to be God's gracious gift to them. The ini-
quity of the Amorites had filled the cup to an evil overflowing.
In fulfillment of a promise made four centuries earlier (Genesis
15:12-21), God was about to bring his people into the land.

And five young women came to Moses to complain that
something was unfair. They had a grievance of gender, a claim
of discrimination that was tied to the fact they were women.
Why should their father's name be lost among the lines of Israel
merely because he had fathered no sons? In the absence of
brothers, these five women pressed for equity in the presence of
the mighty Moses himself.

Nearly thirty-four centuries later, spiritual sisters of these five women are still asking similar questions. They are not as restrained, however.

Some have grown impatient.

Who Are They?

We need to know who these women (and men) are who are asking the questions today. They are more varied than is usually thought.

We have asked a number of Christian friends about their perceptions of the women's movement. We have found that most are unaware how diverse the women are who are speaking today. People seem to know of Gloria Steinem and *Ms.* magazine (but few of our friends admit ever having read a copy). They know of Phil Donahue (but always say they watch his show infrequently.) They know of NOW (and assure us they do not belong) and can identify the letters of the ERA (but usually have not read the twenty-one words of the proposed amendment). In many conversations, we have discovered that the one clear statement that comes through is that feminists are antifamily, antitraditional values, and anti-God.

Those who know of Betty Friedan seem not to be aware of her changing values and her attempts to renew her spiritual roots. They would be startled to hear her say, as we did, that she no longer regards herself as a secularist, an atheist, or an agnostic. She now speaks of herself as embracing again the faith of her ancestors. The surprise is that she says it was feminism that finally led her back when she realized the traditional Jewish concern for justice was what had set her on her course two decades ago.

It is true, as we witnessed, that Friedan's knowledge of the women's movement is significantly more developed than her understanding of Torah and Talmud, but we are impressed that she is seeking religious roots.

There are radicals who advance feminist causes such as those we noted in the previous chapter. There are women who seem to fit the man-hater, bra-burner, media-image of woman rage. There are those who believe themselves to be witches (and who speak of the Salem witch trials as the Puritan response to covert abortion clinics). There are those who exult in lesbianism, who seek to worship the mother goddess, and who speak with utter contempt for biblical faith.

These women do exist. But they do not exhaust the women's movement.

Feminism and Family

There are also moderate, compassionate, loving, family-oriented homemakers who are feminists. These women are concerned that the feminist movement is perceived as inimical to homemaking. As one has written,

> The stereotype, "Woman's place is in the home," was for a long time applied so indiscriminately that the inevitable reaction, while liberating many women from totally unsuitable employment in homes, has robbed many whose natural place *is* there of the dignity and joy they should have in doing the job that is right for them.[1]

Anne Bowen Follis is a pastor's wife who came into the women's movement reluctantly and has remained a wife, mother, and homemaker. As with many of us, she used to begin her remarks with the words, "I'm not a women's libber— but . . ." However, once she began to work openly for women's issues as a housewife, she often met with incredulity. We love the description she gives of a long distance telephone interview that came at the worst possible time—at five-thirty as she was trying to prepare dinner. With her four-year-old making truck noises on the floor, the dog working toward the butter on the table, the seven-year-old insistently looking for *blue* socks, and the two-year-old pulling things from the refrigerator and saying, "Eat, Mommy! Eat, Mommy!," the interviewer began, "First, I'd like to know if you're *really* a housewife."[2]

There are also career women who are deeply devout Christians and moderate feminists. Dee Jepsen's celebrated book,

Women: Beyond Equal Rights, comes out of a lifetime of family oriented tasks as well as significant political and public service activities. She struggles personally with the word *feminism* because of the connotations given it by radicals within the women's movement and by detractors without; but she speaks from a strongly Christian perspective on the needs of women today, as well as the important contributions women can bring to the family and to society as a whole.

Jepsen, former special assistant to the president for public liaison to women's organizations, says:

> Every human being—man, woman, and child— has a need to be valued, to be loved, and to love, to be intimate and open with someone, to share his or her heart's secrets, to be able to let someone know "who he is" or "who she is," to be himself or herself without fear of being rejected.[3]

The point of her book—that which is "beyond equal rights"— is the importance of women knowing the Savior Jesus Christ, the true liberator.[4] Only then will the problem of finding true meaning in life be achieved. There is more to the "problem with no name" than Betty Friedan ever imagined.

Kari Torjesen Malcolm is another example of a moderate feminist. She has given her life to the service of Christ not only as a Christian wife and mother but also as a missionary and as an active spokesperson for encouraging Christian women to seize new opportunities to serve the Lord. Her early experiences as a child in China caused her to face the fact that the slogan, "A woman's place is in the home," is simply not a distinctly Christian approach to life. The binding of little girls' feet in Old China was designed to keep them at home. Malcolm does not demean women who stay at home to help hurting and needy people, but she finds little grace in those who stay at home merely to watch the woodwork or the television.

> Sometimes I wonder if it is going to take the ravages of war to get the modern Christian American

woman out of her home and her preoccupation with
the trivia of housekeeping and hobbies into the hurting world that needs her love and her message.[5]

Follis, Jepsen, and Malcolm are examples of Christian
women who are seeking new ways to reach out beyond themselves to serve Christ. These women have not turned on their
husbands, abandoned their children, or flouted the Scripture.
But they have found there is more to being a Christian woman
today than many traditionalists would have us believe.

Two Kinds of People

One of the things Beverly was quite unprepared for as she
attended a feminist meeting recently was that most of the
women there were married and mothers. She had expected most
to be single, career women. These women were not talking
about how they might shuck their husbands or dump their children; their concerns were about enhancing their marriages and
improving their child-raising.

There is a story told about a certain pollster who liked to
say, "There are two kinds of people in the world: those who divide people into two groups and those who do not." One of the
realities many evangelical Christians have not yet come to grips
with is that women and men may be genuinely saved,
thoroughly evangelical, biblically committed, well taught, and
deeply spiritual (shall we add, God-fearing Americans?)—and,
at the same time, be feminists! For those who have been given a
two-category approach to life, such facts do not compute. They
are true nonetheless.

What we find so compelling in the five daughters of
Zelophehad is that they came to Moses with a genuine grievance, but they came in the context of faith in God, expectant for
justice. Their attitude was humble, their desire was noble, and
their theology was correct. They knew why their father had died;
it was for his own sins and had nothing to do with Korah's rebellion. His name should not be lost, they argued, just because he

had no male issue. His part in the land should not be forgotten; he did have five daughters! But in all of this, they did not go to the goddess; they came to Yahweh through Moses.

Women Clergy

For some people the central issue in the women's movement as it touches religion is women achieving full, active participation in the synagogue or church as ordained clergy. This is a first stage matter, the achievement of full participation, voice, and power.

Jews as well as Christians debate the issue of the ordination of women. Recently we heard Rabbi Laura Geller describe her path to ordination at Hebrew Union College in 1976, just four years after the first ordination ever of a woman rabbi. Her story brought to our minds the Barbara Streisand film *Yentl*, which describes the difficult struggle of a young Jewish woman to be trained and accepted as a rabbi in an all-male *yeshiva* (a Jewish theological school) in Poland in the early 1900s. Christian viewers of this film surely must ask questions about the training and acceptance of women for Christian ministry as they watch this Jewish woman struggle against seemingly intolerable cultural pressures.[6]

While a small number of women have been achieving ordination in some Christian communions for several generations, particularly in Wesleyan and holiness groups,[7] other mainline denominations have only recently admitted women into their ministry rolls. In some of these denominations, a new test question for male ordinands concerns the full and unhesitating acceptance of women ministers. Within these groups a male who is not fully acceptant of women ministers will himself not be ordained.

In contrast, many conservative, evangelical, and fundamental communions will not even discuss the possibility of women's ordination, much less advocate it. This is true as well of many traditional churches such as the various Greek and Eastern Orthodox bodies. Considerable ferment exists among

Roman Catholic religious women for ordination as priests, but little enthusiasm is shown among the curia.

For leaders in these varied churches, the following words of the apostle Paul preclude women from any voice of leadership— indeed, in some cases any voice at all—within the Christian church:

> Wives, submit to your husbands as to the Lord. For the husband is the head of the wife as Christ is the head of the church, his body, of which he is the Savior. Now as the church submits to Christ, so also wives should submit to their husbands in everything (Ephesians 5:22-24).

> Now I want you to realize that the head of every man is Christ, and the head of the woman is man, and the head of Christ is God (1 Corinthians 11:3).

> A man ought not to cover his head, since he is the image and glory of God; but the woman is the glory of man. For man did not come from woman, but woman from man; neither was man created for woman, but woman for man. For this reason, and because of the angels, the woman ought to have a sign of authority on her head (1 Corinthians 11:7-10).

> As in all the congregations of the saints, women should remain silent in the churches. They are not allowed to speak, but must be in submission, as the Law says. If they want to inquire about something, they should ask their own husbands at home; for it is disgraceful for a woman to speak in the church (1 Corinthians 14:33-35).

> A woman should learn in quietness and full submission. I do not permit a woman to teach or to have authority over a man; she must be silent. For Adam was formed first, then Eve. And Adam was not the

one deceived; it was the woman who was deceived and became a sinner. But women will be kept safe through childbirth, if they continue in faith, love and holiness with propriety (1 Timothy 2:11-15).

Likewise, teach the older women to be reverent in the way they live, not to be slanderers or addicted to much wine, but to teach what is good. Then they can train the younger women to love their husbands and children, to be self-controlled and pure, to be busy at home, to be kind, and to be subject to their husbands, so that no one will malign the word of God (Titus 2:3-5).

Silent Submission?

Pretty strong stuff, isn't it? The verses seem to present clear mandates to women: *Submit to your husbands in everything, and be silent in the churches.*

But as we read these verses, do we not also have some questions? For example, is it possible the words from 1 Corinthians 14 concerning the silence of women in the church even call into question the practice of women singing in the congregation? Do not the last words of the quotation from Titus 2 renew for us the claim that the proper place for a woman is in the home, after all? We have heard learned evangelicals say that a woman should not even ask a question in a church business meeting; she should wait and ask that question of her husband in the privacy of their home.

Here is a conundrum. In many churches women are not permitted to teach mixed groups of adults, but are encouraged to teach little children. In addition to the possibility of being out of submission to her husband, the woman teacher of mixed adults may be a teacher of theological error, for "it was the woman who was deceived and became a sinner" (1 Timothy 2:14). Now, if a woman is more susceptible than a man to doctrinal error, why should she be encouraged to teach little children on whom she may have an enormous influence? At least if she were teaching a group of adults, the men would be able to recognize her deception and label it for the error it is. Or is there the fear, as one professor has argued, that the mere presence of her feminine body will divert the attention of the men from their superior theological reasoning abilities so that they will not notice the error at all?

On occasion, women who have been brought up in these churches and who feel the call and gifting of God for Christian ministry, unhappily leave their churches to find other communions where they may pursue their gifting and goals more readily. Some traditionalists term such women rebellious and rejecting of God's authority over them.[8]

New Readings

In the nineteenth century, a significant body of evangelical feminist literature appeared in which the traditional interpretations of the verses we've cited were seriously questioned. This literature suggested that cultural elements prevalent during the time Paul wrote these words no longer persist today.[9] It was particularly in association with the great social movements—the abolition of slavery and the temperance movement—that women in this country began to question the concepts of the submission and silence of women. Further, the great revivals of religion under Charles Finney encouraged women to enter public roles in promotion of their evangelical faith.[10]

For most traditionalists, however, these verses simply may not be interpreted away by resort to culture or expedient. Well-known Bible teacher John MacArthur, for example, says the only way people may argue that women can lead the church and society "is to redefine all the biblical data. . . . I don't believe there's a place for women elders in the church. It is very clear that a woman is not 'to teach or exercise authority over a man' (1 Tim. 2:12)."[11]

We understand the position given by our friend, Dr. MacArthur. It is a viewpoint we have been taught and which we have each taught in the past. It is held by most of the leadership within our denomination as well as our seminary and many sister schools. For our part, we do not wish to muddle our major points in this book by advocating the first stage issues of participation, power, and voice. We believe these matters have been argued well on both sides, and the arguments have continued for over a hundred years. Further, we believe if the issue of women in the church is focused at the first level stage of ordination, the second level issues of relationships will never be dealt with adequately. More women are concerned about the relational issues than are seeking ordination.

We may raise some questions, however, about what the apostle Paul did mean in these several verses we have quoted:

- Do these verses mean the apostle believed women are in some way inferior to men? Before you dismiss this question, be aware that many in the history of the church have concluded this was the intention of the apostle (and the sentiment of God). Church fathers and the great reformers are often quoted in this vein. We do not feel the need to repeat these quotations, any more than we feel the need to quote the fathers and the reformers in their anti-Semitic remarks. It is time for repentance, not remembrance.

- Is it possibly true Paul hated women? Again, many who have read these verses have concluded this is the case. However, we must ask of these people how much they find of hatred in Paul, and how much of their own rage they project to him.

- Is there any way around what seems to be the face-value reading of these verses? Or is even the question of seeking "a way around them" an admission that we have a problem with Paul's negative conclusions and a concession of our desire to escape the implications of such verses today?

- And what about women? What about women who are greatly gifted and able to contribute to church and society, in the home and outside the home? Are women who have taken leadership positions in business, industry, and the community truly rebelling against their God-given nature? Is it really an offense against the spirit of Scripture for a woman to have run as a vice-presidential candidate of a major political party for the first time in 1984? Are countless other women in leadership positions doing what they do in complete defiance of God's will for them?

- Are women who have been spiritually gifted and trained in the ministry of the Word of God only able to function as teachers of little children or of other women? If a woman were to preach the truth of the Word of God to a mixed audience of adults, is that preaching invalidated by her very gender?

- When we admire women Bible teachers instructing men and women in third world countries, but do not let them speak from behind our pulpits here at home, are we not guilty of racism as well as sexism? Or can all this be discounted by the line, "Well, they wouldn't have to do this teaching if sufficient men were to go into world mission"?

- And what about that woman at home whose husband is brutalizing her and her children? Has she no redress? Must she bear all things in silence as she submits to him in everything? Is this her spiritual work, her sharing in the sufferings of Christ?

Cultural Complexities

Our questions continue:

- What about the cultural dimension? It would be difficult to deny that the cultural pattern of the biblical period was patriarchal; but may we still ask if that pattern indicates God's intention for all time, or was it something he worked in and through for his own purposes for his people during that time?

- When we think of the culture of the biblical period, should we not really think of culture*s* and cultural changes? The time period from Abraham of Ur to John of Patmos covers at least twenty-one centuries, the rise and fall of numerous nations, changes of language and geography. Is not the question of biblical culture much more complex than we usually think?

- Further, does not culture work several directions? That is, when we think of the culture(s) of the biblical period, do we not also need to think of the cultural settings and vistas of those who have commented on these texts in the past? Does not our understanding of the text come in part from the cultural vistas of the commentators as well as the text itself?[12]

- And does not our own culture have a major bearing on how we relate biblical texts to our own lives? May not a high view of the providence of God suggest that modern readers must take changes and new realities in their culture into account in dealing with texts such as these?

We will return to some of these issues later in our book At this point we wish only to suggest that there really are significant questions for both traditionalists and feminists to face, and face squarely. To us, the issue of women in church ministry roles does not appear at all to be settled.

An article in a recent issue of *National Geographic* has reminded us of the division of thought among Christian people during the nineteenth century on the issue of human slavery in America. In his article on the Underground Railroad, Charles L. Blockson writes,

Ordeals may have gone unrecorded and names may have been forgotten, but such records as have survived in the memories of men like my grandfather and in the memoirs of those who risked all for freedom and brotherhood make it clear that the flight to freedom on the Underground Railroad was an epic of American heroism.[13]

We well understand the sentiment of this writer. He is the great-grandson of an escaped slave, James Blockson. His grandfather has kept alive the story of the family quest for freedom. Rightly he looks back on his ancestor's escape to Canada as a part of "an epic of American heroism." But was that the viewpoint of the owner of the nonperson/slave, James Blockson, so long ago? Hardly! Doubtless, with the self-assurance of a modern spokesman for biblical morality, that slave owner could quote Scripture texts from both testaments on the immorality of a runaway slave and the criminal system that permitted such to happen.[14]

Times Change

Our culture has changed. There are some people who might still wish to make a case for "biblical slavery";[15] but we suspect most Christian (and non-Christian) readers will rejoice with praise to God as they read the story of the Underground Railroad. It *is* a story of American heroism!

It was only thirty years ago that some southern fundamental pastors were resisting racial integration of their churches on biblical grounds. A few of these pastors have subsequently become nationally, even internationally, known. They include the well-known founder of the Moral Majority, Jerry Falwell, pastor of the Thomas Road Baptist Church of Lynchburg, Virginia, and the great orator-preacher of the largest Southern Baptist church in the world, W. A. Criswell of Dallas, Texas. During the great civil rights movement of the sixties, most evangelical, fundamental leaders of the church were silent; some were openly hostile. Only a few evangelicals dared to link arms with those who may not have had as high a view of Scripture as they in these marches for biblical equity of persons.

But times have changed. People change. People learn. Dr. Criswell himself tells the story—with tears of remorse—of how he has changed the direction of his church so that it is now open to blacks and all people of color. The same is true of Dr. Falwell.

There are Bible scholars of our acquaintance who have spoken angrily against Roman Catholics, particularly during the 1960 presidential election campaign. Pastors have slurred Jews and other minorities from their pulpits to get cheap laughs or, with misguided intention, to make a point. We remember one morning service in a southern city in the early sixties in which we were stunned by the pastor's casual expressions of racial hatreds. This was from a godly pastor of a nationally known church who prided himself on preaching through the Bible year in and year out.

But things change. Fairly recently, a nationally prominent pastor made a stupid, offensive remark about stereotypical Jewish physiognomy. He intended his remark to be a passing joke, but he found that people were no longer laughing. He had to make his public apology known nationally.

Things change.

Do not misunderstand us here. Not all change is for the good. Certainly the prophets of the Hebrew Scriptures did not approve the changes that came into the life of the nations of Israel and Judah when the people no longer worshiped Yahweh. Indeed, at one point the prophet Hosea said of the wickedness of the people of Israel, "they break all bounds" (Hosea 4:2).

Not all change is for the good. Not all things should change.

God does not change. God's character does not change. God's Word does not change. God's truth does not change.

But we change. And our change *may* be for the good. Our values change. Our outlooks change. Our understanding of the Bible changes. Our vistas of God's truth changes. The Spirit of God still teaches.

Is it not possible, in time, that things will change as well in evangelical attitudes toward the role of women in the church? Not because we have capitulated to the evil spirit of the age, but because we have seen a providential work of God just as we have seen in the areas of slavery and race?

Perhaps Not

Perhaps not. *Not all change is for the good.* That is almost a maxim in the experience of Israel in the Old Testament period. Just because something is modern does not mean it is superior.

Perhaps traditionalists will be proven correct after the dust has settled. Perhaps the conclusion of traditionalists that male and female relationships in the church are transcultural, based on the pattern of creation not on passing fads, will be stronger than ever.

Our desire in this area is quite modest, but it may shock some of our friends (and will not satisfy others): *Let's at least keep talking about women and church leadership.* We still have many questions that need to be settled.

Finding Our Way

For most people, however, the issue of women and the church is presented in considerably more modest terms. Most women in our churches are not seeking nor advocating ordination; they are merely trying to find their own way in personal and family relationships. Understanding male and female roles within the family is the real crunch.

Pulitzer prize-winning columnist Ellen Goodman, whose *Boston Globe* articles are widely syndicated, described the sad and touching story of Anita Bryant following Bryant's divorce from her husband Bob Green in 1980. You will remember Anita Bryant's outspoken, active role in opposing homosexuality in Florida in the seventies. Sadly, this activity led to the loss of a national advertising contract, to great personal stress, and finally to the dissolution of her marriage. Goodman's article presents an issue confronting far more women than the question of ordination; it is the concept of wifely submission in a troubled age:

> A few years ago Bryant was questioned about her wifely role in a *Playboy* interview. "If Bob (Green, her husband) asked you to do something right now that was against the grain of your thoughts," she was asked, "would you simply submit to him?"
>
> She answered then, "I might rebel against it—and I have many times—but biblically, I would submit, yes."
>
> But last week, she said no. She would instead divorce her husband after twenty years and four children, because he "violated my most precious asset—my very conscience." Her husband and others, she said, "conspired to control me and use my name and reputation to build their personal careers instead of my ministry."
>
> This woman who once described submission as a choice she had freely made, faced another choice: between her conscience and her marriage, between her beliefs and her husband. It happens, in real life, all the time. . . .
>
> Anita Bryant, too, a public defender of the family and the traditional female role, was pushed or grew out of submission. Hardly a feminist then or now, she has still followed a familiar course: She has chosen her individual conscience over her role.
>
> The lady tried to be a leader in the world and an obedient follower in the marriage. But these are the two ways you can't have it anymore.[16]

How May We Have It?

The problem we all face as men and women in our new world is how *may* we have it? With all the talk of the feminine mystique— and now with charges of chauvinism and counter charges of unsubmissiveness, with talk of the mother goddess, and with prayers beginning "Our Mother who art in heaven"— each of us has to ask new questions and seek adequate direction in our age of turmoil.

These issues do not mean less to those of us who believe the Scriptures really matter. *The issues are more important to us than to anyone*, for they are a part of our whole understanding of who we are as God's creatures, his servants, even the mirrors of his image.

Mahlah and Her Sisters

Remember the story of Mahlah and her four sisters who came before Moses and complained it was not fair their father should have no heir in the land simply because he had no sons?

Here's the amazing thing. When these daughters of Zelophehad came to Moses seeking redress for an inequity based on their gender, the Lord agreed with their complaint! This is what happened:

> So Moses brought their case before the LORD and the LORD said to him, "What Zelophehad's daughters are saying is right. You must certainly give them property as an inheritance among their father's relatives and turn their father's inheritance over to them" (Numbers 27:5-7).

Instead of turning from Father God to the mother goddess or throwing out ancient Scripture for avant-garde heresy, let's follow the lead of these women of so long ago and bring our questions concerning inequity to God and to his Word. This is what we intend to do in the rest of our book. Perhaps we shall be as surprised as they.

Chapter 4, Notes

1. Mary McDermott Shideler, "Introduction," to Dorothy L. Sayers, *Are Women Human?* (Grand Rapids: Wm. B. Eerdmans Publishing Co., 1971), 14.

2. Anne Bowen Follis, *"I'm Not a Women's Libber, But. . . ; And Other Confessions of a Christian Feminist* (Nashville: Abingdon, 1981), 13-14. The warm humor of her book alternates with pain—pain she received from other Christians who are convinced that a woman cannot be truly born again and be active in the support of such causes as the ERA. Much of the feminist movement is called "conscious-raising"; this book ought to be "conscience-raising" for the evangelical reader.

3. Dee Jepsen, *Women: Beyond Equal Rights* (Waco, Tex.: Word, 1984), 86.

4. Ibid., 88.

5. Kari Torjesen Malcolm, *Women at the Crossroads: A Path Beyond Feminism and Traditionalism* (Downers Grove, Ill.: InterVarsity Press, 1982), 186.

6. Stephen Wiest's review of Streisand's *Yentl* in a "Refiner's Fire" column compared the film unfavorably with the Isaac Bashevis Singer story on which it was based, "Yentl the Yeshiva Boy." For Wiest, the film lost the moral and theological subtleties of the original story, leaving only "a black and white view on the issue of women moving into pastoral roles: nobody but a *shlemiel*, fresh from pharisaical prayers thanking God he wasn't born a woman, would ever oppose women's ordination!" "Streisand and Women's Ordination," *Christianity Today*, 10 August 1984, 68.

7. The first ordination of a woman in modern times, according to Nancy A. Hardesty's doctoral research, *Women Called to Witness: Evangelical Feminism in the 19th Century* (Nashville: Abingdon Press, 1984), was of Antoinette Louisa Brown on 15 September 1853 by the First Congregational Church of Butler and Savannah, Wayne County, New York (97).

Hardesty assesses the current situation in this way: "Interest in women's ordination strangely enough, revived in the midst of the 'feminine mystique' of the 1950s. The United Methodist and United Presbyterian churches both ordained women fully in 1956, though there is still strong opposition among some conservative Presbyterians against women pastors and ruling elders. Methodists had given local preachers' licenses to women again in 1919 and ordained them local elders in 1924, but full equality came in 1956. In 1964 the southern Presbyterians followed their northern compatriots. In 1970 the Lutheran Church in America and the American Lutheran Church both ordained women. The Free Methodist Church finally ordained women in 1974. The Episcopal church recognized women deacons on a par with men in 1970 but did not grant women the priesthood until 1976. The first woman became a rabbi in 1972. A few Southern Baptist women have been ordained. However, acceptance by local parishes has been slow, even though as many as 50 percent of the student bodies of some seminaries are women. Holiness denominations still have a much higher percentage of women clergy" (*Women Called to Witness*, 158-59).

As we are writing this book, news has come that the Church of England has made a significant move toward the ordination of women to the priesthood, with the first women expected to take vows as Anglican priests perhaps as early as 1990. ("Ordination of Women Step Nearer," Associated Press story from *The Baltimore Sun*, 16 November 1984.)

Recent books advocating women's ordination include the following:
Paul K. Jewett, *The Ordination of Women* (Grand Rapids: Wm. B. Eerdmans Publishing Co., 1980);

Margaret E. Howe, *Women and Church Leadership* (Grand Rapids: Zondervan Publishing House, 1982);

Judith L. Weidman, ed., *Woman Ministers* (New York: Harper & Row, 1981).

A recent comprehensive study of ordination:

Marjorie Warkentin, *Ordination: A Biblical-Historical View* (Grand Rapids: Wm. B. Eerdmans Publishing Co., 1982).

A series of articles on the function and progress of women in the ministry is found in *Presbyterian Survey*, November 1984.

Solid presentations of a traditionalist view against the ordination of women to the ministry (but which do not limit women from significant ministries):

Susan T. Foh, *Women and the Word of God: A Response to Biblical Feminism* (Grand Rapids: Baker Book House, 1980), 232-58.

James B. Hurley, *Man and Woman in Biblical Perspective* (Grand Rapids: Zondervan Publishing House, 1981).

8. This is the conclusion, for example, of James Kirkland Johnston in his unpublished master's thesis, "A Theological Critique of Evangelical Feminism," (Dallas, Tx.: Dallas Theological Seminary, 1982), 63. This point of view was anticipated by Scanzoni and Hardesty: "Some will argue that change is rebellious, that God has assigned women a subordinate role and made his will for them perfectly clear in Scripture. Women have been protesting such misinterpretations of the gospel since the first century." Letha Scanzoni and Nancy Hardesty, *All We're Meant to Be: A Biblical Approach to Women's Liberation* (Waco, Tex.: Word Books, 1974), 203.

9. A later example of this literary output that is presently available in a new printing is Jessie Penn-Lewis, *The Magna Charta of Woman*; first published in 1919 (Minneapolis: Bethany House Publishers, 1975).

10. Betty Friedan has a chapter in her book, *The Feminine Mystique* (New York: Dell, 1974), that describes the nineteenth century women's movement in America ("The Passionate Journey," 73-94). It did not serve her purposes as a secular writer, however, to present the significant role taken by women of strong evangelical Christian commitment in those years. Nancy Hardesty tells this part of the story in her book, *Women Called to Witness*. In addition to her fascinating text, Hardesty has provided a wealth of bibliographical material, including a listing of nineteenth century defenses of woman's ministry (162-64).

11. John MacArthur, Jr., "Q & A," *Grace to You*, November 1984, 2. Malcolm chafes at MacArthur's strong "women in the home" position. She writes, "He tells women: 'The Bible gives you identity from your children and your family. . . . It's always been that way . . . older women teaching the young women to love their husbands and their children and to be keepers at home.' This man cites one passage in Titus [2:3-5] and cancels all the other commandments given to men and women" (*Women at the Crossroads*, 184-85). Our own view of these verses is that they call for domestic tranquility. These verses by themselves cannot be regarded as a full, biblical statement of femininity—as we shall demonstrate in later chapters.

12. These are issues raised by Cedric B. Johnson, *The Psychology of Biblical Interpretation* (Grand Rapids: Zondervan Publishing House, 1983). Johnson states the theme for his book: "there are no uninterpreted facts in the study of the Bible. 'The Bible says' has been claimed as support for slavery, apartheid, nuclear arms proliferation, sexism, and a host of other unjust sys-

tems. To use fact, theories, and observations to prove a biased perspective is intellectual dishonesty. Differences due to bias among biblical interpreters are not often the result of a conscious twisting of the facts; nor are they due to a lack of scholarship on the part of the interpreter. However, there are some general principles about bias in human perception that apply" (ibid., 10-11).

13. Charles L. Blockson, "Escape from Slavery: The Underground Railroad," *National Geographic Magazine*, July 1984, 9.

14. A convenient presentation of the standard arguments raised by biblically oriented spokesmen for the institution of slavery in the American south is given by Willard M. Swartley, *Slavery, Sabbath, War and Women: Case Issues in Biblical Interpretation* (Scottdale, Penn.: Herald Press, 1983), 31-64.

15. We are distressed that Susan T. Foh seems to do this in her book, *Women and the Word of God*, 31-37. Is it possible that she is unwilling to allow any cultural issue to affect her interpretive process, lest she might be pressed to consider culture in the present discussion?

16. Ellen Goodman, "Anita Bryant: Between Her Husband and Her Conscience," in *At Large*, copyright 1981 by The Washington Post Company. Reprinted by permission of Summit Books, a division of Simon & Schuster, Inc.

PART 2

FINDING THE
BIBLICAL BALANCE

What are the basic issues of women's liberation? Do women want to become men? No, we simply want to be full human beings. In the minds of many, however, only men are human— women are their female relatives. Only men can participate in the full range of earth's activities—women have a "proper feminine sphere." Thus to ask for full humanity is, for many, to "want to be like men." Feminists, however, are not denying the basic biological differences between the sexes. We only ask that these differences no longer be used as the basis for judgments of superior/inferior, dominant/subordinate, wide-choices/rigid roles, vast-opportunities/limited-spheres, and the like. Women are not asking to "become men." We only want to be persons, free to give the world all that our individual talents, minds, and personalities have to offer. Nor are we interested in taking over things or pushing men out of the way. We only ask to be recognized as equal partners, "joint heirs of the grace of life" (1 Pet. 3:7) and "fellow workers in Christ Jesus" (Rom. 16:3).
Letha Scanzoni and Nancy Hardesty
All We're Meant to Be

Chapter 5

The Beginning

*M*ahlah and her sisters had a complaint based on a grievance of gender. They believed their father's memory and his inheritance in the land of Canaan were about to be lost forever simply because he had begotten daughters and no sons. As we have seen, these women brought their complaint before Moses— and through Moses to Almighty God (Numbers 27).

More than three thousand years have passed since these five women questioned the Lord through Moses. Today we have more questions than ever. The very least that we may do is to go back to the text of the Lord that he gave through his prophet Moses and to ask questions about that text, questions concerning its real meaning and abiding value for our living today. Perhaps we may still come as Mahlah and her sisters came, humble and open, yet expecting an answer to our difficult questions concerning male and female issues.

Once, in a Garden

When we think of the biblical story of the garden in Eden, we have several tasks to do. The first is to see what the biblical story really is and what it really says. This is necessary because so many people in our day have conceptions about the garden story that are not at all in accord with the text.

Think back to some of the things said by Merlin Stone about the story of Adam and Eve in the garden. For Stone, the story of Eve was one of the greatest shams in history, a story concocted by willful male supremacists who wished forever to keep women subjugated.[1] For these reasons, Stone argues, the unflattering portrait of Eve was invented: a giddy, flighty girl who was so easily deceived by the serpent, and then the sultry seductress who so smoothly destroyed the noble and able male by her feminine wiles. Thus in the story of Eve, or so we are asked to believe, the two principal errors of the human female are to be found: silliness and seductiveness. "Women!" little boys still hear their fathers say. "You can't live with 'em, and you can't live without 'em!"

Lilith—Adam's First Wife

Even ancient Jewish traditional readings of the story of Eve have led some people to similar negative conclusions. A question came to some ancients: Why was Eve so weak and so wanton? A story grew alongside the biblical account presenting an explanation. According to this extrabiblical, imaginary story, God made another woman before he made Eve. When this first woman, whose name was Lilith, proved to be a disaster, God then made the more passive and compliant feminine model, Eve, as Adam's trusty helper.

Louis Ginzberg summarizes the Jewish story of Lilith this way:

> The Divine resolution to bestow a companion of Adam met the wishes of man, who had been overcome by a feeling of isolation when the animals came to him in pairs to be named. To banish his loneliness, Lilith was first given to Adam as wife. Like him she had been created out of the dust of the ground. But she remained with him only a short

time, because she insisted upon enjoying full equality with her husband. She derived her rights from their identical origin. With the help of the Ineffable Name, which she pronounced, Lilith flew away from Adam, and vanished into the air. Adam complained before God that the wife He had given him had deserted him, and God sent forth three angels to capture her. They found her in the Red Sea, and they sought to make her go back with the threat that, unless she went, she would lose a hundred of her demon children daily by death. But Lilith preferred this punishment to living with Adam. She takes her revenge by injuring babes—baby boys during the first night of their life, while baby girls are exposed to her wicked designs until they are twenty days old. The only way to ward off the evil is to attach an amulet bearing the names of her three angel captors to the children for such had been the agreement between them.[2]

This account of the woman before Eve gives us a projection of what might happen if a woman were really(!) the equal of her mate.

Can't you hear Adam say to her, "Peel me a grape, Lilith." And her response: "Peel it yourself! And while you are at it, where's dinner?"

She would insist on her rights as an equal to him, and if he refused her the exercise of these rights, she would leave her husband to find her "sense of space." One day, like an early Ms. Kramer (remember the film?), she would look for a better life of her own. If need be, she would break religious propriety (pronounce the Ineffable Name of the Lord), be identified with the elements of evil (the Red Sea, an enemy of the Lord), and endure unbearable suffering (the loss of a hundred demon children daily). But she will have her revenge on Adam's children by Eve, the original Other Woman. Godly mothers henceforth need to resort to magic to avert her spell.

Perhaps you are not familiar with the figure of Lilith. If not, you might be as surprised as we were during one seminar session on women in the Bible. At one point, a Jewish woman asked with incredulity, "Where is Lilith?" When someone told her Lilith was not really in the biblical account, she would have none of it. She was sure we had done something to cut Lilith out of the Bible.

Adam's Other Face

Strangely, another old rabbinic idea is resurfacing in our day. This is the concept that when God created mankind he made one creature that was a hermaphrodite, a sexually composite creature. One of the most learned and respected of living rabbis has recently renewed this notion. Rabbi Adin Steinsaltz, whom a writer for *Newsweek* once described as having "the sort of mind that comes around only every couple of thousand years," presented an address to the Lubavitch Foundation in London in July 1984 on the subject, "The Feminine Principle." In that address he said the Lord did not create Eve out of Adam's rib. Rather the Lord created a hermaphrodite being that was then cut into two parts, a male and a female, much like he split heaven and earth in the Creation.[3]

Despite the fact this opinion is presented by a famed rabbi, the concept of the creation of an originally hermaphrodite creature who was subsequently divided into man and woman is certainly not sustained by the Hebrew text. Adam was not two-faced! The Hebrew text clearly states, "male and female he created *them* (Genesis 1:27). The plural pronoun shows that the male and the female humans were separate from each other when God created them, not fused into one being.[4]

Eve's Discovery

Misreadings of the biblical account of the creation of Adam and Eve come not only from the past. There are many misreadings in our own day as well. One of the most common is the presumption that the sin of Eve, and then of Adam, was the discovery of their human sexuality. Many whose knowledge of the Bible is rather informal are sure the real sin of the first couple was sexual in nature. Student Bible knowledge quizzes at the beginning of a course often point this out. There are others who deliberately bring this point of view to the text. For these readers, the "forbidden fruit" was the apple of the sensual desire of Adam and Eve.[5] However, we believe such ideas come more from Greek philosophy than from biblical faith. The result is the same: a denigration of women.

By diverting attention away from pride and the desire to become like God as the essential factor in original sin to sexual intercourse as epitomized in the "seductive" nature of woman, the church has succeeded in legitimizing prideful domination on the part of men and irresponsible submission on the part of women.[6]

"What Are Those Rocks?"

More sophisticated misreadings of the text come from professional Bible scholars whose presuppositions are rationalistic rather than revelational. A current trendy approach to the biblical story of Adam and Eve is to regard the story as an *aetiology*, that is, as a manufactured explanation for conditions which prevailed in the world of the Bible, or those common to human experience.

We may explain the concept of an aetiology in this way. Suppose a child were to ask her daddy why there was such a large stack of stones near the Jordan River. Her daddy, a quick thinker and always one who wished to come up with a fine spiritual lesson, would say: "That stack of stones? Oh, let's see. Years ago, when our ancestors crossed over the riverbed of the Jordan, they crossed over on dry ground. [Pretty nifty, huh? This ties in the crossing over the Jordan to the crossing over the Red Sea. This is going to be one of my best!] Then, when they all crossed over to this side, they took a bunch of stones [No, wait. Let's make this one really good.] . . . they took twelve stones, one carried by a representative of each tribe [This is it! This is my best yet!], and they set up these twelve stones just as you see them today as a memorial to the work of the Lord."

Eventually this story would make the rounds and would become the standard explanation for the pile of rocks near Gilgal on the banks of the River Jordan. Finally, with literary polish and some fine detail work, this story would become a part of the official recital of the history of God's people, which you may read today in Joshua 4:1-9.

A Story to Fit the Case

Sounds farfetched? This is precisely the process suggested by a Roman Catholic scholar as to how the story of Genesis 2 and 3 came to be written:

> What do we know about the actual writing of the account in Gn 2-3? Let us begin with the second scene in Gn 3. Basically, this is a sophisticated reflection and faith understanding of the psychology of human life as the author saw it being lived in his time. To begin at the end, men and woman are conscious of living outside of paradise—to borrow a word, as they themselves did. Men sweat and slave to tame nature and make it fruitful, yet it always fights back and eventually buries them. Women are always drawn inevitably toward men so they can beget children and yet find it pain and frustration. What hurts particularly is that they are dominated by men.[7]

See how it works? The child comes again to her daddy and asks why Mommy cried so much last night when her baby brother was born. And while she was at it, the little girl wants to know why Daddy had to work so hard to make things grow in the field. Daddy was wrong when he thought his story about the rocks at the Jordan was his best. This is an opportunity to give new meaning to the word *best*.

"Well, honey," he begins, "a long time ago there was a man and a woman who lived in a perfect place where no one had to work hard and no one ever cried out at all in pain. No thorns and no screams. [Careful now; let's make this one sing!] Well, one day a nasty old snake came up to the woman and began to get her all confused about herself and God, . . ."

But For Us

So what *do* we have in Genesis 1-3? Is this section of the Bible a sham story invented as an antiwoman tract to keep women in their place? Is it a prim attack on human sexuality? Is it just a part of a longer story of Adam and Lilith, the most interesting part having been cut off? Or is the story ultimately just a creative response to a little girl's question as to why her mother screamed so hard when her baby brother was born?

For us, and we trust for you, the Genesis narrative is none of these things. It is not a tract against either women or human sexuality. It is neither a truncated story nor an account made up to answer a little girl's question. It is, we believe, a revelation from Yahweh through his prophet Moses that presents an accurate and trustworthy account of the formation and early history of our first parents.[8]

Moreover, a careful reading of this section of the Bible is essential for an adequate and balanced view of women and men today. Some books on the biblical perspectives of the "woman question" center in the New Testament problem passages and only mention the Genesis texts in passing.[9] These approaches tend to suffer from a problem in hypothesis testing, moving as they do from the particulars to the general, rather than from beginning with the general concepts and advancing to the particulars.[10]

We believe we need to begin at the beginning.

A Play in Three Acts

The story of Adam and Eve in the garden is a play in three acts, each act taking one chapter in the Bible.[11]

Act I. God creates all of the universe as the setting for his creation of man. When God creates man as male and female he makes them equal and complementary to each other. They are made to mirror the image of their Maker in managing the world in which he is placing them.

Act II. A closer look: God creates man in two stages, the male before the female. For it is he who shall have leadership in their relationship, though she is his equal in every respect. Together in blessed partnership they are to mirror the image of their Maker.

Act III. Trouble in paradise: The human beings God has created to mirror his image rebel against his word by actions of their will, the female first but the male no less surely. God's judgment comes upon both of them, as does his promise of mercy. Now the delicate balance of an ordered relationship of equal persons will be most difficult to maintain, and the act of mirroring the Maker's image will be imperiled as well.

This is an overview of our understanding of male and female relationships in the early chapters of Genesis. Genesis 1 presents the creation story from a grand and awesome perspective: God brings light out of the ominous darkness, dry land out of the watery abyss, an ordered cosmos out of the primeval chaos. His garment was light, the heavens his tent, and the waters were rebuked by his word (Psalm 104:2, 7). Then, when God has made and filled creation, mastered and beautified the universe—*then* it is that God makes mankind. When God made man as male and female, it was as the apex of his wonders.

A right perspective on what it means to be human is possible only with this high view of God's special creation. Witness the pathetic secularism and relativism of the "animal rights" activists, who base their concern for animals on a plea for common worth with mankind. For the antivivisectionists, there is an assumption of arrogance on the part of those who believe people are more significant than other life forms. On a recent "60 Minutes" interview, one activist (a thoracic surgeon, no less) said he did not know of any reason to believe he was more important than his dog. Cruelty to animals is one thing; contempt for the majesty of being human is quite another.

In chapter 1 of Genesis God makes mankind. There is no possibility for one to think the male is superior to the female (or that the female is superior to the male!). Both are made as complementary partners in God's plan for humanity: mirror the Maker in the world he has given, and manage that which he has made for his glory. This point of view presents the highest possible perspective of the wonder of what it means to be human. That perspective, the biblical perspective, is of the woman and the man doing God's tasks together.

Full Human Beings

When Christian feminists say their primary desire is not that women want to become men, but that "we simply want to be full human beings,"[12] they have no stronger base to build upon than the one established in Genesis 1. The high point of Genesis 1 is the creation of man—not man as male, but man as male *and* female.

In His Image

It is man as male and female who is made in God's image:

So God created man in his own image,
in the image of God he created him;
male and female he created them (Genesis 1:27).

The female is as much a bearer of the image of God as is the male. This cannot be stressed too strongly in our day.[13] Genesis 5:1-2 restates the concept that man as male and female both reflect the image of God:

This is the written account of Adam's line.

When God created man, he made him in the likeness of God. He created them male and female; at the time they were created, he blessed them and called them "man."

There is a sense in which the image of God demands both the male and the female partners together for there to be an adequate reflection in his people. This is why one writer has said, "it takes both men and women to adequately reflect God's character. This is one reason, I believe, God told Adam and Eve to become one. Only through a uniting of their two natures could the mother and father of our race truly glorify their Creator."[14]

At the same time, there is a danger today among evangelicals to place too much stress on gender differences; the moment one makes a list of "masculine" or "feminine" traits, generalities become absolutes and subtleties of genuine personality variations are lost. Psychologist Paul Olson speaks for needed caution in this area:

> Gender differences have been vastly overworked and overemphasized. God created male and female differently, but I believe that those differences are so profound and subtle that they have yet to be even partially understood. Most of the gender differences heralded in the Christian media are really only cultural differences. At least by implication, cultural distortions of the male and female personality have been enshrined as God's will in creation. For example, men are consistently found to be "less emotional" than women. After years of working with both, I don't believe it. Men have been conditioned to suppress their emotions and then God has been credited for what is actually an aberration of His original creation.[15]

With His Blessing

It is man as male and female who receives the blessing of God. Genesis 5:2 also picks up on this major factor from Genesis 1. For it was the couple, not the individual, who received blessing from God. Both received the commands to reproduce:

> God blessed them and said to them, "Be fruitful
> and increase in number; fill the earth and subdue it"
> (Genesis 1:28).

The female as well as the male was blessed by God. Nothing in these words may be construed to argue that the blessing of the woman is inferior to that of the man, is conditioned upon the man, is secondary to the man. She is not "womb-man," the mere receptacle for his seed, hiding in the shadow of his blessing. She and he—the two of them together—were blessed by God their Maker.

Further, the two of them together were commanded to reproduce. This factor of the text of Genesis ought to defuse two misconceptions: that human sexuality was the reason for the fall, and that the Bible singles out women as having a primary interest in procreation.

These are real issues and they must be faced squarely. The Catholic scholar who presented the story of the creation account as an aetiology assumed that one of the interests motivating the writer of the stories of Genesis 2 and 3 is the notion that "women are always drawn inevitably toward men so they can beget children."[16] Fischer was developing his aetiology without keeping in mind the balancing words of Genesis 1:28. It is not just that women are drawn to men for the sake of having children; men are also drawn to women for the same purposes. Biblical notions of parenting are balanced. Yet there are other reasons than just the production of children that draw us each to the other. The principal reason we are drawn to each other is because of our humanity in God's image; it is as we are drawn to each other that God makes us one (Genesis 2:24).

The certain teaching of God to our first parents was that they would be parents—together! The words, "be fruitful and increase in number; fill the earth and subdue it," are, as one wag has it, the only command of God man has taken seriously. Yet the point of the passage we wish to stress relates not to the present problems of overpopulation (and underproduction) in some parts of the world; the issue is that these words came from the Creator to the couple together.

With Royal Commission

It is man as male and female who receives the royal commission from God to rule the earth:

> "Rule over the fish of the sea and the birds of the air and over every living creature that moves on the ground" (Genesis 1:28).

The words of this verse are in continuity with the Creator's intention for man announced prior to man's creation (Genesis 1:26). They continue to be God's intention for man long after the fall (see Psalm 8:6-8, where these words are used in slightly new inversions by the great poet David). And these words will finally be realized in the fullest possible measure by the Lord Jesus Christ (see Hebrews 2:5-8, where the words of Psalm 8 are quoted with reference both to man and to the Savior Jesus). In fact, the command "Rule!" is one of the major Messianic roles, as Christ will accomplish what our parents were first commanded to do.[17]

But in their original setting, in the beginning, in Genesis 1:28—these words from the mouth of the Creator God were given to the female and to the male, to both of them together. How may one say that a woman, by virtue of her gender, may not have a position and function of leadership when the mandate from God "Rule!" was given to the woman as well as to the man? Genesis 1 does not indicate any limitation on the woman that is not upon the man as well. They were both made by God as coregents on the earth, to rule together over all that he had made.

And It Was Very Good

The final words of God at the end of the sixth day were said of the female as well as of the male:

God saw all that he had made, and it was very good (Genesis 1:31).

We suspect some readers might wonder why we wish to stress this, but we believe it to be necessary from both the point of view of the text as well as from the negative, patronizing, degrading—and, yes, sinful—attitudes many male believers through the ages have had toward women. If our assertion is true that the high point of the creation story in Genesis 1 is the formation of man as male and female, then the words of God at the end of his creative week are most significant.

The use of the term *good* is impressive in the creation story. It is one of several key words used in the creation story in multiples of seven—a mark of conscious artistry in the writing of the Genesis account. [18]

On six occasions God has declared his creative work to be good:

God saw that the light was good (Genesis 1:4);
God saw that the division of land from sea was good (1:10);
God saw that all manner of vegetation was good (1:12);
God saw that all the stars and heavenly bodies were good (1:18);
God saw that all creatures that fill the waters and fly in the air were good (1:21);
God saw that all the forms of animal life that move about on the earth were good (1:25).

Then it was that God made man, the chef d'oeuvre of his creation, the masterwork of his making; and God made man as male and female. And then God saw that all he had made was very good, exceedingly good, altogether good.

The female as well as the male.
The woman along with the man.

We submit that any debasing language or demeaning attitude toward women, based merely on gender, is an affront to the very words of God their Maker. To speak in a belittling way about women is to attack our common humanity and to slur that which God has said is "very good indeed."

It is for these reasons that we resist any discussion of women's issues that does not begin with Genesis 1. This is where Scripture begins. This is where God has chosen to begin. This is where we must begin.

Moreover, we grieve at the history of misogyny in the synagogue and in the church. Again, it is not our purpose in this book to recite the evil words that have been spoken against women by otherwise great men. Many other books have done this sorry task.[19] We are as loathe to perpetuate these offenses as we would be to present a catalog of Polish jokes in the context of speaking out against the belittling of persons based on factors of national origin. It is enough to say that these egregious statements have been made repeatedly by otherwise godly men. It is time today for godliness to extend to how men think of and speak concerning women.

For it is *with women* that men share the divine commission given to our first parents, to mirror the majesty of our Maker in the world in which he has placed us as his regents.

It is *with women* that men may share the new commission to bring the gospel of Christ to all peoples everywhere.[20]

And assuredly it is *with women* that men may share together in the blessings of the new heavens and the new earth. One day God will dwell again with humanity, but in a manner that will transcend what once was in the garden:

> And I heard a loud voice from the throne saying, "Now the dwelling of God is with men, and he will live with them. They will be his people, and God himself will be with them and be their God (Revelation 21:3).[21]

The allusions in Revelation 21 to Genesis 1-3 are numerous, and John uses great prophetic texts from Isaiah 60 and 65 and Ezekiel 40-48 as well. At the End is all of the promise of the

Beginning. That promise will be realized by people who are truly human in their creation, who are fully liberated in their salvation, and who are female and male in their personhood as they mirror their Maker together.

Our point is this: Genesis 1 presents the strongest possible case for the equality of women and men in biblical theology. The term *equality* should not need a modifier, any more than the word *unique*. But if we must do so in today's debate, we are even willing to bend grammar and say that Genesis 1 presents the *full equality* of women with men.

Many evangelicals have been taught to reject women's liberation and to suspect even biblical feminists. But we do not have to agree entirely with the steps biblical feminists such as Letha Scanzoni and Nancy Hardesty take to get to their conclusion. It may be sufficient for many of us just to find that we understand a little better the direction they are walking when we hear them say:

> We simply want to be full human beings . . .
> We only want to be persons . . .
> We only ask to be recognized as equal partners.[22]

These are the issues of humanity. These are the issues of our creation. These issues are the stuff of Genesis 1.

Chapter 5, Notes

1. Merlin Stone says that her book, "the story of the suppression of women's rites, has been written to explain the historical events and political attitudes that led to the writing of the Judeo-Christian myth of the Fall, the loss of Paradise and, most important, why the blame for that loss was attributed to the woman Eve, and has ever since been placed heavily upon all women" (*When God Was a Woman* [San Diego: Harcourt Brace Jovanovich, 1978], xiii). We have discussed Stone's book more fully in chapter 3.

2. Louis Ginzberg, *The Legends of the Jews* (Philadelphia: The Jewish Publication Society, 1909), 1:65, 66. The force of the Lilith story in later Jewish mystical theology is described by Raphael Patai; in Kabbalistic literature she was said to become the wife of God when the Temple was destroyed (*The Hebrew Goddess* [New York: Avon Books, 1976], 221-25). Some feminists have used the imagery of Lilith to evoke an image of sisterhood to be

found in an old heroine. See Judith Plaskow, "The Coming of Lilith: Toward a Feminist Theology," in *Womanspirit Rising*, eds. Carol P. Christ and Judith Plaskow (San Francisco: Harper & Row, 1979), 206-7.

3. "Famed Rabbi Talks on Women & Judaism," *Portland Jewish Review*, July/August, 1984, 8. As he continued his presentation Steinsaltz admitted that the woman in traditional Judaism has a limited role, but he held out a bit of hope to her in the more civilized age of the coming of the Messiah: "Then the men will have to learn to be quiet."

4. This point was argued long ago by U. Cassuto, *A Commentary on the Book of Genesis, Part I: From Adam to Noah*, trans. Israel Abrahams (Jerusalem: The Magnes Press, The Hebrew University, 1961), 57-58.

5. This is the assumption of Stone who says that it was Eve's "eating of the tree that gave her the understanding of what 'only the gods knew'—the secret of sex—*how* to create life" (*When God Was a Woman*, 217). Hence, sex became "the original sin," and "Judaism, and following it Christianity, developed as religions that regarded the process of conception as somewhat shameful or sinful" (ibid., 218).

6. Margaret Wold, *The Shalom Woman* (Minneapolis: Augsburg Publishing House, 1975), 55. There are places in traditional Jewish writings where Satan's motive in tempting man was his own lust for Eve. See E. Earle Ellis, *Paul's Use of the Old Testament* (reprint; Grand Rapids: Baker Book House, 1981), 61.

7. James A. Fischer, *God Said: Let There Be Woman: A Study of Biblical Women* (New York: Alba House, 1979), 78-79.

8. In considering these chapters as a revelation from the Lord to Moses, we are not at all dismissing the prehistory of the concepts within these chapters either in Hebrew tradition or in the ancient Near Eastern setting in which the Hebrew peoples lived. Valid studies may be made as to the nature and origin of the source materials that the biblical writers used. But the chapters as we have them are now a part of Holy Scripture, and as such, are part of the out-breathing of the Lord in the formation of his word (see 2 Timothy 3:16).

9. Consider Ryrie's well-known treatise, for example, where the only reference to Genesis 1 is to a Midrash on Genesis 1:26 concerning the roles of angels. Charles Caldwell Ryrie, *The Role of Women in the Church* (Chicago: Moody Press, 1958), 74.

10. This is a general criticism of some evangelical tendencies in hermeneutics suggested by Mark Noll, "Who Sets the Stage for Understanding Scripture?" *Christianity Today*,, 23 May 1980, 17; and developed by Cedric B. Johnson, *The Psychology of Biblical Interpretation* (Grand Rapids: Zondervan Publishing House, 1983), 27-30.

11. Actually, the story begun in Genesis 1 extends to Genesis 2:3; the new story in chapter 2 begins with verse 4. Genesis 2:4 itself is a matter of significant debate. R. K. Harrison has argued that this verse is a colophon to Genesis 1 (*Introduction to the Old Testament* [Grand Rapids: Wm. B. Eerdmans Publishing Co., 1969], 544); our approach is to say that this verse is introductory to the new section. As we shall see, our approach has profound implications for the theology of Genesis 2. The heading, "This is the account of the heavens and the earth when they were created," centers exclusively on man as male and female. The creation of man is the point of the creation of the universe.

12. Letha Scanzoni and Nancy Hardesty, *All We're Meant to Be: A Biblical Approach to Women's Liberation* (Waco, Tex.: Word Books, 1974), 206.

13. Some of these concepts are presented as well in Ronald B. Allen, *The Majesty of Man: The Dignity of Being Human* (Portland, Ore.: Multnomah Press, 1983), 81-94.

14. W. Peter Blitchington, *Sex Roles & the Christian Family* (Wheaton: Tyndale House Publishers, 1980), 51.

15. Paul Olson, "Making the Most of Marriage in the 80's," *Virtue*, July/August 1982, 21. We are on much better ground if we speak concerning physiological differences between the man and the woman—beyond the obviously sexual! The experiences of female cadets at West Point over the last several years has given researchers sound data concerning biological sex-related factors. See Barbara Rowes, "Fighting Chance," *Omni*, November 1984, 80.

16. Fischer, *God Said: Let There Be Woman*, 79. This same writer seems to believe that the eating of the forbidden fruit was the discovery of their sexual selves: "Adam and Eve ate of the tree and they did learn how to keep life going; they learned that they were naked and what their nakedness was for" (ibid.). See also note 5, above.

17. See Ronald Barclay Allen, *When Song Is New: Understanding the Kingdom in the Psalms* (Nashville: Thomas Nelson, 1983), especially chapter 10: "A Hymn of Glory: Psalm 110."

18. Cassuto gives these data in an elegant section of his commentary, *Genesis, Part I*, 12-15. The use of the number seven in the wording of Genesis 1 is most impressive.

19. A convenient summary, forcefully presented, is given by Paul K. Jewett, *Man as Male and Female: A Study in Sexual Relationships from a Theological Point of View* (Grand Rapids: Wm. B. Eerdmans Publishing Co., 1975), 149-59.

20. Some readers might object that Matthew 28:16 seems to present the eleven disciples as the only hearers of the words of the so-called "Great Commission." Hence, we suppose one might argue that the Commission was not given to women, as only men made up the band of the eleven. But if one wishes to be so petulant, we would respond: Do you really wish to limit the words of the Great Commission to these eleven persons? Certainly not! The issue is not that they were male; it is that they were the eleven apostles. When the Holy Spirit descended upon the believers who were gathered in Jerusalem on the day of Pentecost, it was women with men who began to speak with other tongues. The apostle Peter aptly attested to these facts when he quoted the prophecy of Joel 2:28-32 to the astonished crowd—a text which speaks of "sons and daughters" and "both men and women" receiving God's Spirit and prophesying in God's name (Acts 2:17-21).

21. Given the confused understanding of the nature of language in our present day, perhaps we should note that the dwelling of God in the future blessed state is not to be with men as males, but with humanity as a whole. It would be sexism of the worst sort not to understand that the term *men* (Greek, *'anthropoi*) in this verse is generic and is inclusive of males and females.

22. Scanzoni and Hardesty, *All We're Meant to Be*, 206.

*Women were not treated as men in the Old Testament.
God created man and woman in his image but for
different functions. The husband is the head of his wife,
and she is his helper; together they are one flesh. After
the Fall, this relationship, both the equality in being
and the inequality in function, is threatened and would
have been lost without God's revelation in the Old
Testament. Consequently, many Old Testament laws
distinguish between women and men to maintain the
husband's headship. The Hebrew woman is also
pictured as a capable and worthwhile being—in
relation to God and to her husband (if she has one). The
Old Testament's teaching about women is not the
prejudice of a patriarchal society.*
Susan T. Foh
Women and the Word of God

Chapter 6

The Beginning . . . Again

G *enesis 2 is worlds apart from Genesis 1.* This most unsettling fact will be very important for us in our continuing study of the male and female issue in Scripture.

So different is Genesis 2:4-25 from Genesis 1:1-2:3 that a whole body of biblical scholarship exists based on the concept that different authors wrote the two chapters. This approach to the Bible, often termed *higher criticism*, has serious philosophical, theological, and methodological errors. But the differences between the two chapters cannot be ignored, even by those of us who follow the traditional view that Moses was the principal author of the Pentateuch. The differences between the two chapters are manifold.

A New Name for God

Genesis 2 uses a new name for God, "the LORD God" (or Yahweh God), whereas Genesis 1 used only the generic term for deity, "God" (Hebrew, *'elohim*). The generic term *'elohim* speaks of the majesty, might, and power of the Creator, and is most suitable for the transcendent wonder of deity in Genesis 1. Genesis 2 uses the personal name for God, Yahweh (sometimes mispronounced "Jehovah").

Yahweh is the name by which God explains his ongoing relatedness to his people, especially in the context of the great deliverance of Israel from Egypt (Exodus 3:12-14), the heart of the gospel in the Hebrew Scriptures. It is most appropriate for God to be described by his personal name in Genesis 2 because of this chapter's description of his close association with his people, the man and the woman he made and placed in the garden. Yet, lest the reader wonder if this is a new deity, the name of God is conjoined to the generic term of chapter 1; hence the Creator is called *Yahweh 'elohim* .[1]

New Perspectives

Genesis 2 gives a new perspective for creation. Whereas Genesis 1 builds gradually to the great climax of the story with the creation of man as male and female, Genesis 2 begins with the creation activities already in process, and moves very quickly to the story of the forming of man. It is this story which occupies the substance of the narrative.

Genesis 2 suggests a new relationship for man as male and female. In Genesis 1 we naturally thought of the creation of the male and the female as one event. We are quite unprepared for the new insights of Genesis 2 that the male was created before the female and that a crisis—the man's aloneness—had arisen before the woman was fashioned from his body. That the female was created later than the male brings questions to our mind as to God's purpose in delaying her formation.

New Point of View

Genesis 2 is informed by a different point of view than chapter 1. In chapter 1 the vista is awesomely grandiose; from some high vantage point in space in the midst of the forming universe, we hear the Creator as he makes each new part of the cosmos by the words of his mouth. In chapter 2 we are on the earth beside the man looking at creation from the level of his perspective. In chapter 2 we see the lushness of the garden, we hear the rush of the rivers, we stand near to ostriches, eye-level with fluttering butterflies.

New Moral Tone

Genesis 2 proceeds with a new moral tone we were not prepared for in chapter 1. In Genesis 1 everything God has made is pronounced by him to be good. There is nothing but supernal bliss. The evaluation God gives of the totality of his own work is that it was completely perfect (as the words, "very good" may be translated).[2]

In chapter 2 some things are found to be *not* good. One is simply not prepared for the mention of the tree of the knowledge of good and *evil* (Genesis 2:9). How could there be this suggestion of evil when everything God has made is good? Moreover, we are startled to read that if one were to eat of the fruit of this tree they would be inviting *death* (Genesis 2:17). Genesis 1 was all about life; Genesis 2 introduces the concept of death. When we look again we find this ominous tree planted in the middle of the garden, a dubious place of honor, right beside the tree of life (Genesis 2:9). These observations are most unsettling.

One more thing is not good: the man God created was alone in the midst of a garden lush with food and teeming with living things; in the midst of Paradise there was not another creature like himself. And God said, "It is not good " (Genesis 2:18).

These things are new to us; Genesis 1 did not prepare us for them. When we look a bit more closely at the record of Genesis 2, we learn some other new things we were not told in Genesis 1.

Adam First, Then Eve

As noted previously, the male was created before the female, and this prior creation gives him some sense of priority over her. It is difficult to say this with sufficient care; the tendency to misstep here is enormous.

What we wish to assert is that the male and the female were not created together, as we would have thought from the first account. That God made the male before the female must be considered seriously in any biblical reckoning of the male and female issue. Certainly the New Testament writers base their understanding on this factor; we may not ignore it.

> For man did not come from woman, but woman from man (1 Corinthians 11:8).
>
> For Adam was formed first, then Eve (1 Timothy 2:13).

This fact is not the whole of the story, but it is a part of the story. And it slips up on us in Genesis 2.

A Rose and a Name

The second fact we observe is that when the Lord made the female and presented her to the male, it was the man who named her. Names bore more significance in the world of the Old Testament than they do in modern Western society. A name was a cipher of being, a symbol of one's meaning. Not only was the name itself important, but so was the giving of a name. In the Old Testament world there was often a sense of ownership or proprietorship associated with naming something.

The first creation story in Genesis 1 shows us the importance of naming. There we see God, who has made the light and the darkness, giving these created works their proper names, "day" and "night" (Genesis 1:5). God, who has created the expanse, gives it its proper name, "sky" (Genesis 1:8). He also names the dry ground "land" and the waters "seas" (Genesis 1:10). He was the proper one to give names to his works, for he had made them and they were his.[3]

Yet, strangely, God does not name the other creatures he makes—beings that fill the seas, that fly in the air, and that move about on the earth. After giving names to day, night, sky, land, and seas, God stopped naming his works—with one exception.

Only one other creature does God name: man. This is implied in Genesis 1:26, "Let us make man in our image, in our likeness." The other creatures God made were of manifold variety, but only the most general language was used of them: living, moving, flying creatures. But for the finest work of God a name came from his mouth: "man." In the Hebrew language of Genesis the name "man" is *'adam*, a word that sounds very much like the word for "ground" *'adamah*. This is fitting, for Genesis 2:7 describes Yahweh God making man from the dust of the ground. Man is of the earth, earthen in his chemical makeup. In this respect, man is like all the other earth creatures God made; they too were formed out of the ground (Genesis 2:19). And when man dies, like the animals, it is to the earth that he returns.

Adam's Names

Whereas God gave names to the day and night, to land and sea and sky, he left it to man to give names to all the other creatures he had made. The language of Genesis 2:19-20 is significant:

> Now the LORD God had formed out of the ground
> all the beasts of the field and all the birds of the air.
> He brought them to the man to see what he would
> name them; and whatever the man called each living
> creature, that was its name. So the man gave names
> to all the livestock, the birds of the air and all the
> beasts of the field.

This was a royal task God gave to the man. He was to name every animal God had made. There is a suggestion of expectancy on the part of God in these verses: "He brought them to the man to see what he would name them" (Genesis 2:19). It is as though the Lord was holding his breath, wondering what the man would do next. But the man did well this royal task. "Whatever the man called each living creature, that was its name" (Genesis 2:19).

When God gave to man this task of naming the creatures, he delegated a royal prerogative to him, an attestation of God's seriousness in forming man to rule over the earth (Genesis 1:28). But God had another point for man to learn, a far greater wonder for man to behold than observing and naming all the animals.

Eve's Name

For these reasons we take most seriously the datum that the man named the woman whom God created after him and whom God presented to him. There are some feminists today who have attempted to evade this issue. There are also some traditionalists who have pressed this too far.

Here is the amazing thing: When the man named the woman it was with a full consciousness that although he was formed first, and although he was exercising a role of leadership in naming her, nonetheless she was from him, she was like him, she was his equal. So the man gave her a name that means the same thing his own name means. His name for her was a happy joke; it was the feminine complement of his own name. These are his elated words:

> This one! This time!
> (That is, At last!—here is one who corresponds di-
> rectly and truly to me!)
> Bone—from my bones!
> And flesh—from my flesh!
> This one shall be called woman
> For from man this one was taken!
> (Genesis 2:23, personal translation)

Alone in the Garden

Imagine what it must have been for Adam at the beginning, before the creation of the woman. Adam was lord. But he was a lonely lord. In a garden teeming with living things, there was no creature that was like him. None could meet his needs for companionship. The apes, the canines, the felines, the great and small bovines—none was like him. Adam gave good names to the animals he studied. He must have observed the taxonomical similarities between himself and some of the animals. But none was like him. Adam was gifted with speech in a world that was speechless. Here he was giving names to creatures, but only the Lord who was waiting expectantly nearby could understand the names, could discern the meaning of his sounds. Of what use to an ape is it to have the name "ape"? Such names are useful only to man, and the man who gave the names was alone.

Doubtless Adam saw and understood the mating patterns of the animals he studied and named. Creatures of all descriptions passed by him in review. Adam saw the males and the females of the great varieties of animals God had made. But for him there was no partner; for him their was no mate. He was lord, but he was an increasingly lonely lord.

And he was looking. This is the point of Genesis 2:20b, "But for Adam no suitable helper was found." Can't you sense his expectation, now heightened, now sagging, as more and more creatures were paraded before him by the Lord? "God is so inventive! So imaginative! So creative! Certainly in all the life forms he has made there will be another like myself," Adam must have thought. But finally the parade was over. At last all the animals had been named. Adam has exhausted his great mind by naming them every one, all creatures great and small, all things bright and beautiful, all life forms strange and ignoble. But there was not one like himself.

Greater Than the Stars

The creation of the woman, therefore, is one of the most touching, most marvelous moments in the entire creation story. When God made the woman he truly made a wonder. The woman was a marvel that surpassed all other life forms; she was more dazzling than the very stars!

The ancients worshiped the stars; many moderns still do. The lofty language of Genesis 1 passes off the creation of the stars almost as an afterthought: "He also made the stars" (Genesis 1:16). By that short sentence, the majesty of the Creator is demonstrated in a magnificent manner. For the pagans who might read such words, and for those in the covenant community who were so prone to adopt the paganism of their neighbors, these words cut away all the power and the supposed dignity of the stars. "As for your supposed gods, O deluded ones of the nations, God made them as well."

When God made the stars, we might have expected all the music in heaven to ring out. Yet only a brief sentence is allotted the stars' creation. But when God made woman, that is when the music began to play. For the creation of the woman has been built up by suspense, wonder, and surprise. Do we not join Adam in his exuberance as he says, "This one! This time! At last, one like myself"?

Does the second creation story degrade woman? Not at all! Only a deliberate misreading of the text of Scripture would lead one to think that women are degraded in Genesis 2. The creation of woman is *celebrated* by the writer of Genesis. God's creation of her is the high point of the passage.

Civility and Celebration

How do our conventions of gentility relate to the worth of women? Are these demeaning? Some of them probably are. For example, we read about the after-dinner tradition of wealthy families a generation ago where the men would retire to the study for cigars, drinks, and serious conversation. The women were expected to stay in the dining room and chatter about girl things. The modern Christian equivalent is found in countless church socials. When the meal is over the men gravitate to one side of the room and the women to another. The men talk about serious issues (football?), and the women chatter about trivial things (children!).

We have always resisted this approach to Christian socializing for two reasons: we enjoy sitting together and do not wish to pass up any chance to do so, and we find the discussions of mixed groups generally more interesting.

What about the convention of a gentleman opening doors, helping with wraps, and holding chairs for a woman? Scanzoni and Hardesty feel these things have to go in the new world in which we live.

> The end of male chauvinism will also mean the
> end of chivalry in the traditional sense of men con-

tinually smoothing the way for the "weaker sex." Women can no longer expect doors to open, seats to become vacant, packages to be carried for them simply because they're women.[4]

We have a different approach to these things, for we do not believe the concepts of civility need to be regarded as demeaning to women. When a man opens a door for a woman, he is not necessarily putting her down as too weak and frail to open the door for herself. Rather, the man may in fact be celebrating the woman in a fashion that recapitulates the feelings of Adam toward Eve.

Don't you think that had there been doors in the garden, Adam would have opened them all for Eve, made each one a revolving door for her? His joy at finding one who was like himself must have been boundless! Open doors? He'd climb the highest mountain for her, swim the broadest sea for her, catch a falling star for her.

Opening doors, pushing up chairs, and holding wraps are just tokens of man's joy that there is a creature so wonderful as woman. It is a celebration of woman who is the long-awaited equal partner for man. Those women who do not wish to have these little civilities done for them are missing out on part of the celebration of being a woman genuinely appreciated by a man. These civilities do not put women down; they mark them out as special. They say nothing about frailty; they point to joy. They do not suggest the woman is inferior; they add to the celebration begun by Adam at the beginning of time: "This one!—at last— This time!" Come on, Letha and Nancy. Join the party. You may enjoy it again.

Headship and Equality

In Genesis 2, then, we learn new complexities in the relationship of women and men. The man has a certain headship over the woman because he was created before her and he names her. But this headship is in accord with their mutuality and equality. We cannot forget the lessons of Genesis 1 when we come to Genesis 2, unless we wish to divide the word of the Lord wrongly.

In many ways, Genesis 2 is a different world than Genesis 1. *Yet Genesis 2 is the same world as Genesis 1*. There is a new name for God, but it is the same God. There is a new perspective on creation, but it is the same creation. There is a new order to the creation of the man and the woman, but they are the same persons. The new world is the same world though it is seen from a different perspective.

When we read these two chapters, we need to see how they fit together. Both are a part of the Word of God, and that Word is noncontradictory. Further, these chapters are placed together at the beginning of the Bible. Those readers who insist Genesis 1 and 2 do not agree and impute two sources for them must have a low regard for the intelligence of the scribes who supposedly put them together. If the differences are truly irreconcilable, would not the ancient scribes have seen that as well? It is inconceivable that two chapters—the very first two chapters!—of the Bible might be greatly contradictory and be side by side. The strongest reason for us to look for harmony in these two chapters is their proximity.

Equality . . . Inequality

Hence, whatever chapter 2 says about the headship of the man cannot be read as inferiority or inequality for the woman. We find it difficult to follow the approach Susan Foh has presented, even though she attempts to state her position with care. Foh describes the relationship of the man and the woman as one of "equality in being but inequality in function."[5]

Inequality is inequality. Unequal is unequal. Foh's language here is an unnecessary slanting of the case. It is preferable to say that the Bible presents the woman as the full equal of the man without presenting a concept of equality that means interchangeability. The woman is the equal of the man, but is not interchangeable with him. We are dealing with people, not with mathematics. But the stress needs to be placed today on the issue of equality, simply because it has been ignored or abused for so very long.

Factors of Equality

Genesis 2 reaffirms the basic equality of the woman and the man that we already have found in Genesis 1. Here are four salient factors:

- The intention of Yahweh to make a helper suitable for the man (Genesis 2:18), shows that the woman is the man's equal in the divine perspective;[6]
- That the woman was taken from the man (Genesis 2:21), shows she is of the same essence as he;
- That the man gives the woman a name comparable to his (Genesis 2:23), shows he recognizes in her his equal;
- That the narrator concludes that the two of them become "one flesh" (Genesis 2:24), shows they are equal in their persons.

Hence, *Genesis 1 and 2 present a complex picture of a delicate tension between equality and headship*. The man has a certain priority over the female, but she is his equal in every way. To speak of functional inequality is to bring more (or should we say less) to this text than the text will bear. The emphasis is rather on the fact that the man, who does have some priority (which we may call "headship" on the authority of the New Testament epistles), finds in the woman a full complement of himself.

The Fall

We need to add one more element: the story of the fall. This is the third act of the drama begun in Genesis 1. It is in the fall of man that the delicate balance between man as male and female came into jeopardy. The fall broke the relationship man as male and female had with God the Creator. The fall resulted in pain and thorns, in sin and death; it also brought strife between the woman and the man that continues to our today.

Radical secular feminists hate the story of the temptation, for they argue it is this chapter that has brought such harm to women through the centuries. But the negative views of women said to come from Genesis 3 must come from some sort of hearsay and not from a close reading of the text. For in the text itself, Eve is not presented in the drastically negative light so many seem to suppose.

A Play on Words

The story begins with a subtle pun, based on the words *naked* and *crafty*. The last words of Genesis 2 read:

> The man and his wife were both naked, and they felt no shame.

The first words of Genesis 3 read:

> Now the serpent was more crafty than any of the wild animals the LORD God had made.

The Hebrew words *naked* (*ᶜarummim*) and *crafty* (*ᶜarum*) sound very much alike, and they tie the two chapters together.[7] The naked innocence of Adam and Eve is contrasted brilliantly with the malevolent shrewdness of the ill-defined evil one.

We understand by the last words of chapter 2 that the man and the woman were fully comfortable in each other's presence in their innocent state, and that they had a completely full relationship with each other in all areas of life, emotional, intellectual, spiritual, and—assuredly—sexual. We resist strongly any suggestion that the discovery of sexuality was the occasion of the fall of man. Such a point of view is a slur on the Creator as well as a fundamental misunderstanding of human sexuality as something essentially sordid.

The word *naked* usually brings to us associations that are untoward, secret, and perhaps scandalous. For these reasons, the words "and they felt no shame" are so very significant. They remind us of the words of the New Testament that the marriage bed is pure (Hebrews 13:4), and they also point us forward to the delicious exuberance of true biblical sexuality as found in the Song of Songs.[8]

The Serpent and the Woman

The beginning of the third chapter is ominous. In the words that describe the serpent we are introduced to a great mystery in Scripture: the source of evil in the good universe God had made. The serpent too is one of God's creatures. But this one is "crafty"—the word speaks of an inversion of wisdom, of the dark side of knowledge. It was this serpent, whom we believe to be an incarnation of Satan,[9] that came to the garden and brought about sin, rebellion, and ruin in man.

Much is made of the fact that the serpent came to the woman and began his assault on her. Some have argued the serpent would not have been so successful had he attempted to deceive the man instead. This approach is fruitless for at least two reasons: (1) The text does not indicate any reason for the serpent to come to the woman rather than to the man; hence, any explanation we give is speculative; and (2) though the woman does commit the sin of rebellion before the man does, she does not go down without an argument. The man, however, gives in without a word. Rather than accuse the woman of being a silly little thing who, upon realizing her sin, becomes the femme fatale, the siren seductress who destroyed the man, is it not more in line with the story to say she at least tried to reason with the serpent? Adam in this chapter is something of a wimp. He doesn't say a word, just opens his mouth and eats.

In the Bushes

Contrast the responses of the man and the woman when the Lord approached to speak to them. As Yahweh came near the human couple on whom he had lavished all the bounty of the garden, they were hiding in the bushes with the coverings of fig leaves they had made for themselves. With their pitiable discovery of the dark side of wisdom, nakedness, which had once marked their innocence and bliss, was now a shameful reminder of "their openness of guilt before God."[10] Sin turns things inside out; the very best becomes the worst, the pure is defiled, the lovely ruined.

Were the story not so fundamentally tragic, it would be comic. Two little naked people trying to cover themselves like awkward adolescents caught in an embarrassing indiscretion, and hoping to hide from the Creator of the universe! Thousands of years would pass before David would describe the silliness of trying to hide from God:

> Where can I go from your Spirit?
> Where can I flee from your presence?
> If I go up to the heavens, you are there;
>   if I make my bed in the depths, you are there.
> If I rise on the wings of the dawn,
>   if I settle on the far side of the sea,
> even there your hand will guide me,
>   your right hand will hold me fast.
> If I say, "Surely the darkness will hide me
>   and the light become night around me,"
> even the darkness will not be dark to you;
>   the night will shine like the day,
>   for darkness is as light to you.
>   (Psalm 139:7-12)

Noble Adam

But trying to hide behind the bushes in their Designer's leaves was not the worst thing our first parents did that day. The worst thing was done by Adam when he tried to blame God for his own evil action! He reasoned that, after all, God had given him the woman and it was all the woman's fault. Listen to the exchange:

> But the LORD God called to the man, "Where are you?"
> He answered, "I heard you in the garden, and I was afraid because I was naked; so I hid."

And he said, "Who told you that you were naked? Have you eaten from the tree that I commanded you not to eat from?"

The man said, "The woman you put here with me—she gave me some fruit from the tree, and I ate it" (Genesis 3:9-12).

As we read these words are we not struck by the man's futile attempt to escape responsibility for his action? He ate without a word, but he whimpers when caught with the pulp in his beard.

The Woman's Story

And the woman? When she is asked by God to explain her action, she does not seek to shift blame as the man did. She gives a straightforward account of what had happened:

The woman said, "The serpent deceived me, and I ate" (Genesis 3:13).

In these words the woman confesses her great sin in a simple and direct manner. Some have felt that she too passes the blame. But she does not charge either God or Adam with her fault. Her words are accurate and sufficient. We find it difficult to find anything in this account that belittles her, that demeans her, that treats her with less dignity than the man.

The plain fact is that both the man and the woman committed a terrible breach of trust with Yahweh, a breach that has affected all of human history. From that time to this we are all under sin. From that time to this mankind commits sin. From that time to this people die in sin. The act of treachery done by our parents was no little thing. This was no sneaking cookies from the cookie jar.

But in this terrible act, there is no demeaning of the woman. She was the first to sin, but she was not alone in her sin. And given the way each committed their sin and the way each responded to God about their sin, in some ways the woman comes off looking a bit better than the man.

The Curse

The most important consequence of the sin of our parents as it affects the relationship of man and woman is found in the curse the Lord gave to the woman. The verse is a familiar one to all who have grappled with the struggle of the sexes.

> To the woman he said,
> "I will greatly increase your pains in childbearing;
>   with pain you will give birth to children.
> Your desire will be for your husband,
>   and he will rule over you" (Genesis 3:16).

This verse speaks of two maledictions that come into the woman's life because of her part in the rebellion against God in the garden. First, childbearing will now be a blessing fraught with pain. We may presume from this verse that the bearing of children might have been accomplished without the pain that so regularly attends birthing. We do not know what the physiological (or psychological) dimensions might have been, but the concept of pain in childbearing is presented here as something new in the postfall world.[11]

Birth Pain

Two things we may observe about this factor. First is the simple recognition that one of the most fundamental characteristics of being a woman, the ability to bear children, was affected by the fall. It is not that the woman would be unable to bear children; rather, during this time of unmitigated joy there is now a passage of pain. The pain is not only physical; some women face great postpartum emotional stress as well. We suspect most every woman can relate to these things, whether she has borne a child or not. Today, thanks to more permissive regulations in maternity rooms (one of the good benefits of the women's movement), the father is able to be there with his wife and to share in some way her experience.

Of our four children, Ron was only able to be present in the room for the birth of Rachel, our youngest. It may sound audacious, but Ron took along the movie camera, with the doctor's permission. The very finest home movies we have are the ones from that hospital delivery room. The lighting was fine, the shots were clear, the lens was in focus, and the camera did not malfunction. Our finest home movies, and we can only show them at home!

As we have watched this film on a number of occasions as a family, we have all been impressed with the scenes showing Bev's face just before and just after delivery. It is hard to imagine such a contrast—perhaps one of the sharpest contrasts of expression humanly possible within such a short span of time. Her face was transformed from a look of deep stress in hard work (no wonder they call it labor!), to an expression of exquisite delight—all in a manner of moments. No one who has been present with his wife at such a moment can call her "the weaker sex."

This is a part of our legacy from our first mother.

Relieving Pain

The second observation about pain in childbirth is that it is not an affront to God for a woman to do those things that may help to alleviate the pain or to prepare her to endure it. This needs to be said even today, we have found, because some deeply spiritual husbands fear their wives are sinning if they try to deaden the pain. All this verse says is that childbearing will now be accompanied with pain. It does not say a woman may not seek some method of dealing with that pain. Think of the curse on the ground that came because of the sin of the man (Genesis 3:19). The fact that work needs to be done now with sweat and toil and that the ground will bear thorns along with produce has never kept a farmer from using labor saving devices and weed killing implements. It is as right for a Christian woman to go to a Lamaze class, for example, in preparation for childbirth as it is for her husband to use a power mower on the back lawn.

Her Desire

Genesis 3:16 speaks of two problems that come into the woman's life because of her part in the sin against Yahweh. The first is pain in childbearing. The second is found in these words:

> Your desire will be for your husband,
>   and he will rule over you.

We believe Susan Foh has done an inestimable service to the church in helping us understand these words in a new way. Instead of expressing the woman's sexual desire for her husband (an unlikely result of the fall!), the *desire* spoken of here is a desire to usurp his leadership. That is, in addition to pain in childbearing, the curse on the woman produces conflict between herself and her husband. We do not follow Foh in all of her conclusions, but are grateful to her for pointing out the way for us to interpret this verse. [12]

Breaking the Balance

Because the man was created prior to the woman and because he gave her her name, he exercises a level of headship over her. But his headship is within a relationship of equals, for Genesis 1 has displayed that both the woman and the man are bearers of the image of God, both are rulers over the earth. Mutually they share the tasks of sovereignty and majesty to the glory of God.

This suggests a delicate balance: the woman is equal to the man, but the man is the head of the woman. With the fall, that delicate balance is lost. Now the woman resents even his loving headship, and the man responds as a brute, putting her in her place. Her desire is to lead the relationship; his is to lord it over her.

Ephesians and Genesis

This approach to the delicate balance of Genesis helps us better understand Paul's words in Ephesians 5. These words, so often used to "put women in their place," really address the whole postfall relationship between women and men. To the woman, whose postfall tendency is to usurp her husband's headship, the apostle says, "Wives, submit to your husbands as to the Lord" (Ephesians 5:22). And to the husband, whose postfall tendency is to stomp and to snort, the apostle says, "Husbands, love your wives, just as Christ loved the church and gave himself up for her" (Ephesians 5:25).

Thus the words of the apostle that have troubled so many readers are words of comfort to people caught in the postfall relational imbalance between women and men.

The fall did not, as some have supposed, bring about the headship of the man. Those who speak this way claim that the Christian woman, now rescued from the fall, is no longer to consider herself under the headship of her husband, for Christ has delivered her from that. After all, "There is neither Jew nor Greek, slave nor free, male nor female, for you are all one in Christ Jesus" (Galatians 3:28).

Christ and Design

We have argued that the loving headship of the husband was a part of God's original design for the man and the woman in the garden. This is not something Christ has done away with; rather, in him this headship is again made right.

Think again of Paul's words in Ephesians 5. It is *in Christ* that the woman submits to her husband, and it is *as Christ* that the husband loves his wife. Christ did not come to destroy God's pattern for the woman and the man. He came to make that pattern work again. Indeed, Christ came that the pattern might work *even better than in Eden*. In Eden there was not the knowledge of the love and the life of the Savior Jesus that we have today.

Mutual Submission

The exciting thing about Ephesians 5 and 6 is the appearance of the unexpected. We should not be surprised to find commands given to wives (Ephesians 5:22-24), children (Ephesians

6:1-3), and slaves (Ephesians 6:5-8), for these commands might be thought to perpetuate expected standards of behavior. What is quite unexpected is that those regarded as superiors in each pair of relationships are also given commands. Husbands are taught to love their wives (Ephesians 5:25-33), fathers to nurture their children (Ephesians 6:4), and masters to treat their slaves favorably (Ephesians 6:9). These are countercultural commands; these are unexpected words.

Further, we find that the lead sentence for the paragraphs on relationships is one of *mutual submission*: "Submit to one another out of reverence for Christ" (Ephesians 5:21). This verse colors all that follows. The verses that speak of the wife submitting to her husband (Ephesians 5:22-24) are in the context of the lead verse that demands submission by all. This means the godly Christian husband will at times submit to his wife, not because he is weak but because the love of Christ so constrains him it is not necessary to effect the macho image he once thought made him a man.

The headship of the husband is the general biblical pattern. This goes back to Genesis 2 and is clearly taught by Paul and Peter in the epistles. But the husband is the head of an equal. The more he realizes her true dignity, worth, and wonder, the more he will consult with her, discuss with her, and—when she points the way—follow her. Why not? For the genuinely biblical husband believes as much in the equality of his wife (Genesis 1) as he does in his headship over her (Genesis 2).

A Beginning

These are the genuine beginning issues for man as male and female. We believe all the biblical teaching concerning women and men is in agreement with the concepts first presented in Genesis 1 through 3—in fact, may be traced to there. Whatever progress we make today with one another has to be done in the light of the teaching of these seminal chapters.

Repressive attitudes toward women come often from people who begin other than at the beginning. We would not think of preparing an entree by starting somewhere near the end of the recipe and hoping it will turn out all right. Learning to live together as women and men is far more difficult than preparing even a special dinner. It is also considerably more important.

Let's begin right by beginning at the beginning.

Chapter 6, Notes

1. Cassuto has developed an insightful guide for the nuances the reader may glean based on the terms used for deity in the Pentateuch. His approach is a stimulating corrective to the standard higher critical fare which posits Genesis 1 as a "P" document and Genesis 2 as "JE." See U. Cassuto, *The Documentary Hypothesis: Eight Lectures*, trans. Israel Abrahams (Jerusalem: The Magnes Press, The Hebrew University, 1961), 31-32. He observes that "Yahweh" will be used when the writer wishes to stress the personal character of the Lord, and when the writer notes his direct relationship with human beings and in moral contexts.

On the meaning of the name "Yahweh" and the confusion concerning the spelling/pronunciation "Jehovah," see Ronald B. Allen, "What Is in a Name?" in William F. Kerr, ed., *God: What Is He Like?* (Wheaton: Tyndale House Publishers, 1977), 107-27.

2. So Gerhard von Rad, following the German theologian Otto Procksch, in *Genesis: A Commentary*, trans. John H. Marks (Philadelphia: The Westminster Press, 1961), 59. Von Rad adds: "When faith speaks of creation, and in so doing directs its eye toward God, then it can only say that God created the world perfect."

3. After saying that in giving "day" and "night" their names there is a mark of essence, von Rad continues: "But in the ancient Oriental view the act of giving a name meant, above all, the exercise of a sovereign right (cf. II Kings 23:34; 24:17). Thus the naming of this and all subsequent creative works once more expresses graphically God's claim of lordship over the creatures" (ibid., 51).

4. Letha Scanzoni and Nancy Hardesty, *All We're Meant to Be: A Biblical Approach to Women's Liberation* (Waco, Tex.: Word Books, 1974), 207. They do go on to call for mutual courtesy and consideration to all persons.

5. Susan T. Foh, *Women and the Word of God: A Response to Biblical Feminism* (Grand Rapids: Baker Book House, 1980), 88.

6. It has long been recognized that the term "helper" (Hebrew, ^{c}*ezer*) is not itself a demeaning word (see, e.g., Scanzoni and Hardesty, *All We're Meant to Be*, 26). People have brought to this word a second-level meaning that has colored the word unnecessarily bleak for women. Moreover, the Hebrew expression translated "suitable for him" (*kenegdo*) speaks of one who is "as his side." That is, the language that has so often been thought to be negative (c.f., the wrongheadedness that has developed concerning "helpmate"), is in fact most positive respecting the person of woman. See Ronald B. Allen, *The*

Majesty of Man: The Dignity of Being Human (Portland, Ore.: Multnomah Press, 1984), 90, 91, and note 10 on p. 94.

7. See Ronald B. Allen, Word Studies 1692 and 1698 in *Theological Wordbook of the Old Testament*, eds. R. Laird Harris, Gleason L. Archer, Jr., and Bruce K. Waltke (Chicago: Moody Press, 1980) 2:695, 697-98. In subsequent notes, this work is abbreviated *TWOT*.

8. A point developed more fully in Allen, *The Majesty of Man*, 135-42.

9. Von Rad writes, "Throughout the entire story this antagonist of man remains in a scarcely definable incognito, which is not cleared up" (*Genesis*, 85).

10. Carl Schultz, Word Study 1588, *TWOT*, 2:656.

11. Just as there is a significant play on the Hebrew words "naked" and "crafty" in this section, so is there a delicate paronomasia between the Hebrew words "pain" and "tree." See R. B. Allen, Word Study 1666, *TWOT*, 2:688.

12. Susan T. Foh, "What Is the Woman's Desire?" *Westminster Theological Journal* 37 (Spring 1975): 380-81. Her argument depends on a new direction for the etymology of the Hebrew word translated "desire" and on the amazingly close congruence of the wording of Genesis 4:7b to Genesis 3:16. For comment, see Allen, *The Majesty of Man*, 144-49. A critique of Foh's position is given by Michael F. Stitzinger, "Genesis 1-3 and the Male/Female Relationship," *Grace Theological Journal* 2 (Spring 1981): 23-44.

*There is neither Jew nor Greek, slave nor free, male
nor female, for you are all one in Christ Jesus.*
The Apostle Paul

*A man ought not to cover his head, since he is the image
and glory of God; but the woman is the glory of man.
For man did not come from woman, but woman from
man; neither was man created for woman, but woman
for man.*
The Apostle Paul

Chapter 7

Balance in the Bible

W e use a brand of shampoo in our home that has a curious note in its required list of ingredients: "Contains Natural and Other Ingredients." What a strange expression. The list begins with water (sounds natural) and follows with innumerable unpronounceable words, none of which sounds natural at all. The clincher, following many polysyllabic terms, is the statement: "May Also Contain the Following," and then some more dubious items are listed. Perhaps we should change brands.

Natural and Other, and Perhaps Something Else Again. This description seems also to apply to the way some people interpret the Bible. There is that which is Natural. There is the Other. And there is the May Also Contain.[1] This mixed-potion approach to the Bible is seen especially when people come to debatable issues, or to the study of concepts on which the Bible seems to present mixed messages.

Cheers . . . ?

A prime example is the subject of wine. Some passages in the Bible speak strongly against the use of wine; others speak of wine as a gift of God. Psalm 104, for example, speaks of wine as one of the evidences of the hand of God in the blessings of creation:

> [He makes] wine that gladdens the heart of man
> (Psalm 104:15).

But just as one is about to raise a glass for a toast, someone quotes Proverbs 20:1,

> Wine is a mocker and beer a brawler;
>   whoever is led astray by them is not wise.

He lowers the glass and sputters a bit.

If we turn to the prophets we find the same duality. One of the most scathing texts in the prophets on the scandalous sins of the wicked priests and false prophets of Israel centers on their drunkenness (Isaiah 28:1-8). The revolting picture the prophet presents is something out of a temperance lecture. The leaders of Israel are staggering and reeling, stumbling and befuddled, their tables fouled with the filth of their disgusting excess. It is an awful sight!

As one is about to "take the pledge," he comes to a passage of exquisite beauty where the same prophet describes wondrous millennial blessings under the Messiah. Here the prophet couples wine with milk as good foods for the delight of the soul, the richest of fare (Isaiah 55:1-2).

Tendenz

How does one put these contrary pieces together? Shall one make a toast or take the pledge? One of the factors that will contribute to the interpreter's success or failure is how much of his procedure is Natural and how much is Other and May Also Contain. We have a friend, for example, who comes to the wine passages with a certain *Tendenz*, a disposition to make all the evidence point in one direction. For him, every passage that speaks of wine in a negative sense clearly speaks of a fermented beverage. But those texts that speak well of wine are descriptive of nonfermented grape juice. God, he avers, could never condone the drinking of real wine. It does not matter that the same Hebrew words are used in each type of text; for this scholar the issue is clarified simply by the point of view in a given passage: "If God approves of the beverage, read 'grape juice'; if he condemns its use, read 'wine.'"[2]

The tendency to come to the Bible with a point to prove, rather than to seek the balance of the Scripture, marks regularly the dispute concerning "the woman question"—*on both sides*.

Those who challenge the traditionalist approach concerning women are often guilty of this mixing of the Other with the Natural in their interpretations. This is to be expected since they really do have something to prove against the establishment opinions. Generally speaking, a "new" interpretation of the Bible is likely to be strained. Hence, one of the things that has cast strong suspicion among evangelicals against the various aspects of the women's movement has been the disdain some feminists have toward the Scripture, and the cavalier attitudes others have had in their interpretations of the Scriptures.

New Texts . . . New Views

We expect a poor attitude toward the Bible among secular feminists, for the integrity of the Scriptures is not their concern. We are still surprised at times at how Scripture fares with these advocates. Secular feminist Gloria Steinem, for example, displays a profound ignorance of scriptural issues when she suggests there are first century manuscripts of the teaching of Christ that are "less patriarchal" than the teaching found in the gospels.[3] By this remark Steinem has indicated that she has no real concept of either the teaching of the Lord Jesus in the Scriptures, which is most positive indeed toward women, nor any real understanding of the preservation and transmission of that teaching. Her absurd remark about "first century manuscripts" would be laughable, were it not so characteristic of a certain mindset.

Another approach to the Scripture was given to us by a feminist who teaches religion courses at a prestigious liberal arts college in our area. She is well-trained in religious studies and could not be caught with the solipsism of Steinem. Instead, her approach is to accept and promulgate those passages she believes affirm women. Those passages, however, that she believes are negative toward women she rejects and ignores. She believes this to be her mandate as a *feminist* religion professor.

Robbing Paul to Pay . . . ?

Another feminist writer has taken a novel approach to the problem of the Pauline passages that speak of the subordination of women, and which feminists believe to be in conflict with his statement in Galatians 3:28, the feminist *Credo* of equality. William Walker has determined that there are critical grounds for rejecting all of the problematic passages; none is the writing of the apostle Paul. Hence, the only genuine Pauline statement we have on the subject of women is Galatians 3:28, a text "which insists on absolute equality in Christ."[4]

Robin Scroggs does a similar number on the Pauline passages. He discards Ephesians, Colossians, and the Pastorals as non-Pauline. First Corinthians 14:33b-36 is a gloss, not a genuine writing of Paul. Only 1 Corinthians 11:2-16 remains as a text from Paul, but he judges this text rather harshly:

> In its present form this is hardly one of Paul's happier compositions. The logic is obscure at best and contradictory at worst. The word choice is peculiar; the tone, peevish. All these difficulties point to some hidden agenda, hidden probably to the Apostle himself as well as his readers."[5]

In a companion article, Scroggs says the controverted passages were written by those who wished to make Paul's teaching conform with the official teachings of the church. Paul is not the antifeminist he is believed to be; his students put words in his mouth, as it were. So Scroggs is able to come to this final assessment: "Paul is the one clear and strong voice in the New Testament speaking for the freedom and equality of women."[6]

One wonders why the later hands that so muddled the epistles with fraudulent statements of the apostle did not simply cut out the offending egalitarian phrasing from Galatians and be done with it.

It is a standard observation in scholarship that the strength of a theory will be seen by how it handles contrary evidence. How strong is a position that simply dismisses the contrary passages as inauthentic?

Equality . . . or One?

Yet, even if we were to grant Walker's or Scroggs's proposals, we wonder if Galatians 3:28 says quite what feminists claim. Here is the verse:

> There is neither Jew nor Greek, slave nor free,
> male nor female, for you are all one in Christ Jesus.

This powerful verse is not in a tract on the male/female relationship, but is an important part of the context of Paul's great teaching on God's justification of sinners by grace through faith in Jesus Christ. The teaching of Galatians 3:28 is not that slaves were no longer slaves, but that slaves were *one* with the free—in Christ. Paul is not asserting that a Jew ceases to be a Jew or that a Gentile ceases to be a Gentile when he or she comes to Christ, but rather that in Christ they are all *one*.

Nor, do we believe, is Paul intending to deny the distinctions between male and female, for these distinctions began with creation: "male and female he created them" (Genesis 1:27). But in a world of distinctions and divisions, categories and slots, superiors and inferiors, lords and toads—in such a world there exists a new world where whoever you are or whatever you are, you are *one* with all who are in Christ Jesus. This is revolutionary indeed! It may not please Gloria Steinem's agenda, but if she would hear it with understanding, it will change her life.

In the Family

Evangelical feminist writers cannot find so facile a solution to problem passages in the Word of God as secularists and religious liberals. But they have their moments as well. And these moments concern us when the persons casting judgment on the Bible claim to speak for the evangelical faith. We also wish to be careful ourselves. In what follows we sincerely do not wish to offend sisters and brothers in Christ.

Virginia Ramey Mollenkott is a well-known evangelical feminist who has expressed what we believe to be a less than satisfactory approach to the authority of the Scriptures. In an intriguing interview by John Alexander in *The Other Side*, Mollenkott demonstrated that her first commitment is to feminism, not to the Scriptures. Here is her own record of her pilgrimage as a Christian feminist:

> If you're interested in my own pilgrimage on this, for years I didn't look too closely at what the Bible says about male-female relationships. I assumed female subordination and tried to live accordingly. I was afraid that if I studied the topic I would see a God who is so unjust to my sex that I would have to give him up, and I couldn't do that. My love for Christ was so in my bloodstream that I couldn't live without him. So I didn't let myself study those passages. . . .
>
> I was into the feminist movement from a secular point of view, but I had been afraid to look at the Bible.[7]

We wish to be charitable to Mollenkott, for some evangelicals have bristled at these words and have not tried to understand her point. We do not fault her for coming to feminism from secular persuasion. Frankly, we believe that if feminism is a valid point of view, it does not matter where it originates. Most of us have learned mathematics from a "secular point of view." Further, we believe her when she speaks of her early commitment to the Lord Jesus Christ and when she says she cannot live without him.

But Something Else Again comes into play when she describes her hesitation to find out what the Bible says about men and women. She had not been prepared to commit herself to the authority of the Scriptures—whatever they taught. When a Christian comes to accept a given point of view from secular culture, a most rigorous study of Scripture is required to bring that point of view under the judgment of the Bible—for good or ill. Her indecision in this regard is most troubling indeed.

It is also symptomatic, we are afraid. Other evangelical women and men have taken a feminist position that transcends their commitment to the authority of Scripture. It comes in varying ways—but this weakness is found all too often.

Paul Versus Paul

We may point to the celebrated case of Paul K. Jewett who found it impossible to reconcile the apostle Paul's statements about male-female relationships. On the one hand, Paul speaks clearly of female subordination to the man (as in 1 Corinthians 11:9), and he speaks as well of the equality of the sexes (as in Galatians 3:28). Jewett analyzed Paul's opinions as a contrast between his old training as a rabbi and his new insights as a Christian theologian:

> The apostle Paul was the heir of this contrast between the old and the new. To understand his thought about the relation of the woman to the man, one must appreciate that he was both a Jew and a Christian. He was a rabbi of impeccable erudition who had become an ardent disciple of Jesus Christ. And his thinking about women—their place in life generally and in the church specifically—reflects both his Jewish and his Christian experience.[8]

Jewett believes there is no way these two concepts of women can be brought together:

Because these two perspectives—the Jewish and the Christian—are incompatible, there is no satisfying way to harmonize the Pauline argument for female subordination with the larger Christian vision of which the great apostle to the Gentiles was himself the primary architect. It appears from the evidence that Paul himself sensed that his view of the man/woman relationship, inherited from Judaism, was not altogether congruous with the gospel he preached.[9]

In his approach to the issue of women in the teaching of the New Testament, Jewett has not brought to bear the inspiration and divine authority of the Word of God. He has rather pitted one text of Paul against another, pointing to the all-too common human foible of self-contradiction. At the same time, we have only Jewett's own decision that Galatians 3:28 is "better" than 1 Corinthians 11:9 as our guide for truth in the epistles. This is judging Scripture by the spirit of the age.

Such tactics can go both ways. In a context of patriarchy (say, Saudi Arabia), would not one argue that the subjection view is preferable (even more biblical!) and that Paul erred in Galatians 3:28 in his enthusiasm for a new sense of equality in Christ?

Jewett is forced to say that he believes the apostle Paul is in error when he speaks of subordination of women in 1 Corinthians 11:7, based on Paul's early, faulty understanding of Genesis 2:18-23:

Is this rabbinic understanding of Genesis 2:18f. correct? We do not think that it is, for it is palpably inconsistent with the first creation narrative, with the life style of Jesus, and with the apostle's own clear affirmation that in Christ there is no male and female (Gal. 3:28).[10]

Tilt!

Most evangelical readers of Jewett's words concerning "error" in the epistles of Paul will have a buzzer going off in their minds signaling "tilt." In our opinion, Mollenkott gets the same tilt buzzer. When John Alexander pressed her as to why a back-to-the-Bible approach will not work with the female-male issue, she responded: "The problem is mostly with the way the apostle Paul deals with women in the church. There are flat contradictions between some of his theological arguments and his own doctrines and behavior."[11]

Thus, the problem is not with our understanding of the text nor with how we relate the texts to each other. Mollenkott places the blame squarely: the apostle Paul was a slow learner. It is too bad for us and for the entire course of church history that he was writing the Scriptures while he was in the learning process![12]

Mixed Signals

In the approaches taken by Jewett and Mollenkott we have examples of those who are unable to come to grips with mixed signals in the Bible.

Actually, there are numerous places in the Bible where mixed signals appear. Some are so familiar we may have forgotten them. One example is the prophetic injunction against sacrifice.

> For I desire mercy, not sacrifice,
>> and acknowledgment of God rather than
>> burnt offerings (Hosea 6:6).

One might wish to say that there is a terrible problem in these words, for they seem to be in direct contradiction to the teaching of Moses on sacrifice. The whole book of Leviticus and considerable sections of the rest of the Pentateuch concern themselves with sacrifice as the will of God for his people. Is Hosea pitting himself against Moses? Is the prophet in error in saying that God does not want sacrifice and burnt offerings from his people?

Or is there a way for us to see that Hosea's intention in reporting these words of God is to affirm the underlying truth of Moses? Is not sacrifice without mercy and burnt offering without acknowledgment of God worthless? Is not Hosea (and the other prophets who say much the same thing) getting at the underlying issues? We believe a careful reading of Deuteronomy 6 and 11 will confirm that the prophet Hosea was not a revolutionary but a reformer.

Kings and Thrones

Another mixed signal concerns the intentions of the Lord for the institution of the monarchy in Israel. Deuteronomy 17:14-20 contains a prophetic word regarding the establishment of the monarchy in Israel and God's desires for a godly king. Yet when the people do clamor for a king, as Moses said they would (Deuteronomy 17:14), the judge and prophet Samuel reluctantly accedes to their request (1 Samuel 8; cf. 1 Samuel 12) and warns of troubles to come upon the nation because of their desire to be like the nations round about them.

In some ways the quest for a king is considered a curse, a rejection of the Lord (1 Samuel 8:7). Yet God's finest prophetic words during the time of the monarchy were given to David the king in blessing his reign (2 Samuel 7:1-17). Some might read these words and argue that kingship was a perpetual evil in the sight of the Lord; others might argue that God's best for Israel is found in his kingdom promises.

Is it not a better approach to try to see the balance in these contrasting ideas? On the one hand, the concept of a monarchy "like the nations" (Deuteronomy 17:14; 1 Samuel 8:5) was a path of ruin and was exemplified in the rule of Saul. Yet, God's purposes for Israel were to be realized in his own king— David, a portent of the coming King (2 Samuel 7:8; Psalm 2:6). That is, we may look for ways to see the harmony in the mixed signals of the Scripture *if we have an underlying conviction that the Word of God is without error or contradiction* (see Psalm 19:7-9).[13]

Pro-Woman Scriptures

We find the approach of Jewett and Mollenkott commend-able when they seek a reasoned explication of the "pro-woman" passages. They are particularly strong, for example, when they speak of the way Jesus affirmed women in his public ministry and in his private life. In fact, we believe the ministry of Jesus to women to be one of the most important aspects of the whole question, and will return to it in the next chapter. In our opinion, many traditionalists have not yet fully come to grips with the startling actions and words of Jesus respecting women. We would have ceased to spout Bunkerisms about women long ago if we had paid sufficient attention to the teaching examples of our Lord.

But we find the approaches of our brother and sister to be seriously wanting when they resort to the question-begging technique of dismissing contrary evidence as though it were the fourth ball for a juggler—too much to handle. [14]

Higher Criticism

Another tack taken by some evangelical feminists in dealing with biblical passages that seem to undercut the points they wish to make is to cast suspicion on the integrity of these passages by invoking a higher critical opinion. Scanzoni and Hardesty do this to Genesis 2. Here is a curious bit of reasoning indeed for women who claim to be presenting "a biblical approach":

> According to biblical scholarship, the second chapter [of Genesis] is older [than the first], imbedded in Jewish folklore from more primitive times. Genesis 1 is a more recent attempt to counter some of the more anti-feminine and anthropomorphic interpretations which chapter 2 had occasioned. [15]

Not only is their position suspect when they try to cast questions on the biblical authority of Genesis 2, based on the presumed time interval between putative JE (Genesis 2) and P

(Genesis 1),[16] but Scanzoni and Hardesty have also presented a most novel reason for the P source to write Genesis 1: he (she?) intended the first chapter of the Bible to be a profeminist tract! One has to ask where they got this inside information. Moreover, the enormity of their charge against the integrity of Genesis 2 is increased when one reads the footnote where they link the teaching of Genesis 2 to the Jewish folklore of Lilith.[17] In a game of hardball, this is a real curve!

When charges are brought that such approaches undercut the authority of disputed biblical texts, Mollenkott says we need to face up to the human weaknesses of Paul:

> It seems to me far less detrimental to the authority of Scripture to recognize that some of Paul's arguments do reflect his human limitations, just as the imprecatory Psalms which express David's vindictive hatred of his enemies are reflections of David's human limitations.[18]

Jesus Versus Paul

There is one more off-speed pitch in the hardball of feminism: press the teaching of Jesus as superior to that of Paul. This was the approach of a well-known lay theologian, President Jimmy Carter, when he argued in support of the Equal Rights Amendment on 24 March 1979 in Elk City, Oklahoma:

> I think if one reads different parts of the Bible you can find a good argument either way. . . . I know that Paul felt that there ought to be a sharp distinction between men and women and women's role ought to be minimal. But I have a feeling that Christ meant for all of us to be treated equally, and he demonstrated this in many ways.[19]

That is, if all else fails, undermine the authenticity of the problematic text as a way of getting away from its presumed teaching. And, by a strange alchemy, the dross in the epistles turns out to be the precious metal: by facing the Bible as it is (with its contradictions), we honor it the most!

No!

It is for these reasons that many traditionalists have said they cannot support feminism. Dallas Theological Seminary professor A. Duane Litfin has written several articles in which he demonstrates the insufficient biblical commitment of leading evangelical feminists. His conclusion is that traditionalists simply cannot follow these feminists because of their weak position on the Scriptures.[20]

The Normal, Other, and Something Else approach to the interpretation of Scripture is not a monopoly of feminists, of course. Some articles written from a traditionalist point of view proceed as firmly in their directions as do the feminist articles in theirs, without really listening to the genuine issues feminists have presented. Our feelings (admittedly subjective) in reading these articles is that the writers were already convinced of their opinions and were then marshaling their best arguments from the Scripture to prove their point.[21]

The strong advantages of the biblical traditionalists, however, are that they do not attempt to undercut the authority of the texts they cite, and they are writing within a doctrinal tradition that is long and stable.

Paul and the Rabbis

When we turn to the New Testament passages that cause such difficulty for biblical feminists, we find them somewhat one-sided, though not without the biblical balance we have discovered in Genesis. Paul is accused by some feminists of misreading the Torah or of basing his opinions on his faulty rabbinic training rather than his new insights in Christ.

These charges are unfounded. Paul's interpretation of Genesis 2 is not misinformed at all. He is quite correct in observing that the woman was made by God after the man, and that implications of headship proceed from that factor of human experience. This was a point we also discovered in the text of Genesis 2. Our discovery does not make the apostle correct; we are delighted that his words approve our own.

Paul does not base his opinions on faulty rabbinic thought. His early years of training as a rabbinic scholar under Gamaliel have left their marks on him, of course. When it suited his advantage, he would stress his Pharisaic tradition (Acts 23:6-10). But the apostle Paul deliberately distances himself from the errors of his early rabbinic training:

> For you have heard of my previous way of life in Judaism, how intensely I persecuted the church of God and tried to destroy it. I was advancing in Judaism beyond many Jews of my own age and was extremely zealous for the traditions of my fathers (Galatians 1:13-14).

But now he had a new teacher, the Lord himself. So Paul says of his gospel:

> I did not receive it from any man, nor was I taught it; rather, I received it by revelation from Jesus Christ (Galatians 1:12; cf. 1:15-24).

False Charge

The charge that Paul's interpretation of the Old Testament was compromised by his earlier rabbinic training is countered both by his own negative language concerning the controversies of traditional rabbinic studies (Galatians 4:9; 1 Timothy 1:4; Titus 1:14; 3:9) and by the futile attempt to find in his writings the types of hair-splittings that the rabbis engaged in. (We should probably say "rock-splitting," for a principle of rabbinic interpretation reads: "A verse is capable of as many interpretations as splinters of a rock crushed by a hammer, for Jeremiah 23:29 says, 'My word is like a hammer that breaks a rock in pieces'" [Sanhedrin 34a].) We look in vain in the writings of Paul for mention of a hermaphrodite beginning for man, or of a

Lilith who preceded Eve, or of any of innumerable false trails that may be found in rabbinic lore.[22]

The apostle Paul, as other writers of the New Testament, did at times cite an Old Testament passage to prove a point (and be directed rightly by the Spirit in doing so), but in that quotation he may not have had in mind the task that confronts us—to explain or expound as fully as possible the teaching of that Old Testament passage in its original setting. We do not expect biblical exposition in these cases, only the use of biblical citations.

Paul's selective use of the material from Genesis was to serve his purposes in the context of argumentation. His intention was not to give us a full commentary on the entire passage. In this way, we may say that Paul is one-sided at times for he does emphasize the hierarchical elements (which we also find) in Genesis 2. Yet Paul does not ignore totally the balancing thoughts of equality between the sexes.

Veils and Angels

Let us now look briefly at these several texts and make a few observations.

First Corinthians 11:2-16. The issue of this section is propriety in worship. The problem was fraught with cultural overtones,[23] but the principles Paul calls upon to advance his argument are rooted in the account of God's creation of man as male and female. The question of the veil for the woman in prayer or prophesying has caused continued controversy,[24] but the passage ultimately demonstrates the biblical balance of male and female relationships: the man does have headship over the female based on the order of creation, but shares as well a mutuality with her—and the two of them together are dependent upon the Lord.

Paul's emphasis in this text is upon the headship of the man because this suits the point he wishes to make. When he speaks of the man as "the image and glory of God" and the woman "as the glory of man," he is not denying her worth or image-bearing; he is affirming that she was created by God but that her creation followed that of the man. But every man has also come from a woman, so there is a balance in their relationship.

In our day, without wishing to risk the excess of some feminist writers, we may do well to emphasize the element of equality this passage presents. In a context that depends upon hierarchy for the apostle's argument to work, we are most impressed with his stress on mutuality.

> It is most important to note that, whatever strictures he may lay upon worship praxis, Paul affirms an overriding principle of equality. This is a unique insight of his religion, for it is *in the Lord* and because *all things are from God*.[25]

As for the angels? Paul's words "and because of the angels" (1 Corinthians 11:10) are among the most perplexing in the New Testament. (It may be that phrasing such as this is designed not only to keep women veiled in public worship, but scholars burdened in their studies!) But it appears Paul's intention is to remind us of spiritual realities that attend not only our walk (Psalm 34:7), but especially our worship. The presence of the angels (and the glory of God they adore!) lifts the discussion of propriety in worship from academic and practical levels to the sublime.

Submissive, as the Law Says

First Corinthians 14:33b-36. Here again, the situation concerns propriety in worship, but the focus is upon women speaking during the worship services rather than on how they were dressed. Paul's words for these disruptive women are stern indeed,

> As in all the congregations of the saints, women should remain silent in the churches. They are not allowed to speak, but must be in submission, as the Law says (1 Corinthians 14:33b-34).

This highly controverted passage seems to present an absolute prohibition of women participating vocally in the worship services of the church. We wish to be cautious here; the obvious meaning may well be the true meaning.

Yet, in this selfsame epistle women are given instructions as to their proper demeanor in praying and prophesying—both speaking functions. Hence the direction of the passage may well be limited to the immediate context: a description of disorder in the exercise of spiritual gifts within the church. The section begins, "When you come together, everyone has a hymn, or a word of instruction, a revelation, a tongue or an interpretation" (1 Corinthians 14:26).

Kari Malcolm's parents, missionaries in pre-Mao China, found that the uneducated women had never been taught to listen. Her suggestion seems plausible that the specific problem in the open meetings of the early church was the chaotic chatter of the women:

> If we allow that Paul may have been using the word [*laleō*, "to speak"] in the sense of babble or inattentive talking, the passage would imply that the problems in Corinth were similar to those my parents faced in China. Paul was not taking away the freedom to pray and prophesy which is implied in 1 Corinthians 11:5, but he is dealing with excesses which occurred as a result of that freedom. In the process of determining the letter of the law in 1 Corinthians 14:34, we should not miss the point of the epistle, which expresses freedom while trying to correct libertinism.[26]

Paul told the women to be silent on the basis of "the Law" (1 Corinthians 14:34). While some have thought it possible that "the law" here relates to customs of the day or to distortions of biblical law, it seems better to point to the general teaching of biblical Torah as Paul's intent. There is no passage in the Torah that says "women are to be silent"; but there are texts that at least imply the phrasing, "[they] must be in submission." Paul's thought in citing "the Law" is probably the implications of Genesis 2, which he has already indicated in his instructions for

148   Finding the Biblical Balance

coverings on the woman's head.

In any event, we find in this passage much the same type of situation that occurs in 1 Corinthians 11. A cultural issue (the chattering of [uneducated?] women in the open worship services) was distracting, bothersome, and disgraceful. The biblical issue to which Paul appeals to restore order is the hierarchy of male and female relationships, coming from Genesis 2. The subordination of the woman is not the only teaching of Genesis 2; but it is the issue that fits Paul's intention in this text.

Silent and Submissive

First Timothy 2:9-15. In some ways this is the most difficult text in the Bible on women and men's relationships. It appears to present an absolute, categorical prohibition of women speaking in any teaching role in the church. It has been understood that way by the larger number of Christians through the history of the church, and the seeming face value of a text is not to be despised just because of the press of contemporary issues or for a desire to be modish.[27]

At the same time, it is possible that there is in this text a combination of cultural and noncultural elements, as we have suggested in the problematic texts in 1 Corinthians. We do not offer a final solution here; we only suggest a crack in the door.

Our clues come in Paul's command that women dress modestly (1 Timothy 2:9-10) and in his demand that women be silent, with his argument based on the deception of Eve (verses 11-15). We find no convincing reason for Paul on a whim to single out Eve as the sole guilty party in the garden; in Romans 5:12-21 Paul has made a strong case for the guilt of Adam. Paul's commands in this section may have been precipitated by wanton actions of certain women teachers, whose dress and demeanor were suspect and whose teaching was heretical.

When Paul speaks to the issue of dress and deportment, it is not a rejection of beauty, hair styles, or fashion that he presents, so much as a call for decency. (The same is true of 1 Peter 3:2-4.) The force of Paul's words may suggest that women were dressing in such a manner as to occasion lust on the part of men, rather than with thought to spiritual worship of God.

When Paul calls for silence, it is not that his desire is for the women to remain ignorant, but that they learn "in quietness and full submission." The term for "authority" (*authentein*) at the very least speaks of "lording it over" the men in the worshiping community.[28] But it is possible that this rare word, as an extension of thought from the brazen manner of dress discussed in the preceding verses, may suggest a vulgar approach to men in the congregation.[29]

Taking this lead, we may assume that in the city of Ephesus there was a potential for tremendous negative influence from the mystery cults which were so attractive to women, and that Paul was directly countering their influence by demanding modest dress and silent learning among the women.

In whatever way we decide the passage is best to be understood, it is possible to see within this text a balance between cultural issues (silence) and normative principles (submission).[30]

When Dust Settles

As we said earlier, it is possible that after all the dust has cleared, the traditional understanding of this passage (and the others like it) will be further solidified as demanding a prohibition of women in teaching ministries over men in all periods and places of the life of the church.[31] It is our suggestion at the present time that this is a premature decision; we wish to keep the discussion open.

In the meantime we will stress the biblical balance: Man and woman have an essential equality as bearers of the image of God, but display a priority of relationships based on the details of their creation by God.

However we decide to interpret these difficult New Testament passages, we need to be aware of the possibility of the Natural, the Other, and the Perhaps Also elements in our practice of interpretation. The one good thing about our shampoo at home is that it has a label, imprecise as it is.

Chapter 7, Notes

1. It is the "May Also Contain" quality that Cedric B. Johnson wishes to alert us to in his book, *The Psychology of Biblical Interpretation* (Grand Rapids: Zondervan Publishing House, 1983). He argues that "our unconscious mental sets and responses can interfere with the quest for the meaning of the Scripture" (118).

2. Robert P. Teachout, *Wine, The Biblical Imperative: Total Abstinence* (Columbia, S.C.: Richbarry Press, 1983), 61. John A. Witmer observes that Teachout's position "is essentially a presupposition imposed on the evidence rather than a conclusion validly drawn from it." Review in *Bibliotheca Sacra* 141 (October-December 1984): 368.

3. Gloria Steinem, *Outrageous Acts and Everyday Rebellions* (New York: New American Library, 1983), 287.

4. William O. Walker, "1 Corinthians 11:2-16 and Paul's Views Regarding Women," *Journal of Biblical Literature* 94 (March 1975):109. A rebuttal to this position is presented by Jerome Murphy-O'Connor, "The Non-Pauline Character of 1 Corinthians 11:2-16?," *Journal of Biblical Literature* 95 (December 1976): 615-21. See also H. Wayne House, "Paul, Women, and Contemporary Evangelical Feminism," *Bibliotheca Sacra* 136 (January-March, 1979):41-42.

5. Robin Scroggs, "Paul and the Eschatological Woman," *Journal of the American Academy of Religion* 40 (1972):284. The hidden agenda, Scroggs suggests, is homosexuality. See comments by A. Duane Litfin, "Theological Issues in Contemporary Feminism," in *Walvoord: A Tribute*, ed. Donald K. Campbell (Chicago: Moody Press, 1983), 338-39.

6. Robin Scroggs, "Paul: Chauvinist or Liberationist," *The Christian Century* 89 (1972):309.

7. John Alexander, "A Conversation with Virginia Mollenkott," *The Other Side*, May-June 1976, 25, 26.

8. Paul K. Jewett, *Man as Male and Female: A Study in Sexual Relationships from a Theological Point of View* (Grand Rapids: Wm. B. Eerdmans Publishing Co., 1975), 112.

9. Ibid., 112-13.

10. Ibid., 119.

11. Alexander, "A Conversation," 22.

12. It goes nearly without saying that Mollenkott's position, and that of Jewett, is out of sync with the position of biblical inerrancy. She admits this: "Paul's interpretation also leads to serious trouble for anyone who believes in inerrancy" (ibid., 28). But then she backs off a bit: "But I hesitate to say that this record of Paul's position is an error in Scripture. It is just an honest record of a human being thinking out loud and working through his conflicts" (ibid.).

13. See Ronald B. Allen, *Praise! A Matter of Life and Breath* (Nashville: Thomas Nelson, 1980), 139-46.

14. Mollenkott is most troubling to us when she denegrates the Hebrew Scriptures. At one point she says, "We could always sort of shove the Old Testament onto the Jews or their theological infancy" (Alexander, "A Conversation," 29.) In these words she smacks of neo-Marcionism, the worst of red

flags to a Hebrew prof—or his wife! See John Bright, *The Authority of the Old Testament* (Nashville: Abingdon Press, 1967), who writes, "there are many of our people who never heard of Marcion and who would be horrified to learn of the company they are in but who nevertheless use the Old Testament in a distinctly Marcionist manner. Formally, and no doubt sincerely, they hail it as canonical Scripture; but in practice they relegate it to a subordinate position, if they do not effectively exclude it from use altogether" (74).

15. Letha Scanzoni and Nancy Hardesty, *All We're Meant to Be: A Biblical Approach to Women's Liberation* (Waco, Tex.: Word Books, 1974), 25.

16. In the standard literary analysis of a certain type of biblical scholarship (which is repudiated by most evangelical scholarship), the major sources of the Pentateuch are believed to have been compiled over a period of a millennium, beginning at a time considerably distant from Moses:

The "J" (Yahwist/Jahwist) source is dated c. 850 B.C.
The "E" (Elohist) source is dated c. 750 B.C.
These sources "JE" were brought together c. 700 B.C.
The "D" (Deuteronomist) source is dated c. 621 B.C.
The "P" (priestly) source is dated c. 440 B.C.

Hence, when Scanzoni and Hardesty speak of biblical scholarship which suggests that Genesis 2 is older than Genesis 1, it is to this theory they are subscribing. Without explaining the implications of their nearly casual statement, these writers do not really alert the unwary reader of the great significance of their implications. Conservative evaluations of the "Documentary Theory" are readily available. The best include the standard introductions to the Old Testament by Gleason L. Archer, Jr. and Roland K. Harrison, plus Kenneth A. Kitchen's *Ancient Orient and Old Testament* (Chicago: InterVarsity Press, 1966).

17. Scanzoni and Hardesty, *All We're Meant to Be*, note 2, 211-12; we have discussed Lilith briefly in chapter 5.

18. Virginia Mollenkott, "Women and the Bible: A Challenge to Male Interpretations," *Mission Trends No. 4: Liberation Theologies in North America and Europe*, eds. Gerald H. Anderson and Thomas F. Stransky (Grand Rapids: Wm. B. Eerdmans Publishing Co., 1979), 224-25. For a superior approach to the genuine difficulty of the imprecatory Psalms, see J. Carl Laney, "A Fresh Look at the Imprecatory Psalms" *The Bib Sac Reader*, eds. John F. Walvoord and Roy B. Zuck (Chicago: Moody Press, 1983), 115-25.

19. News report by Wesley G. Pippert, *Christianity Today*, 4 May 1979, 48, cited by Willard M. Swartley, *Slavery, Sabbath, War and Women: Case Issues in Biblical Interpretation* (Scottdale, Pa.: Herald Press, 1983), 150. Mollenkott places the pattern of Jesus as the bottom line as well. In attempting to find which passages of the Bible are merely the record of erroneous pilgrimages, she says: "Another guideline is the analogy of what Jesus said and did. If something doesn't fit the life and teaching of Jesus, again I know which is for all time" (Alexander, "A Conversation," 75).

20. In addition to the article mentioned in note 5, above, see A. Duane Litfin, "A Biblical View of the Marital Roles: Seeking a Balance," *Bibliotheca Sacra* 133 (October-December 1976):330-37; "Evangelical Feminism: Why Traditionalists Reject It," *Bibliotheca Sacra* 136 (July-September 1979):258-71. Other important traditionalist articles include Bruce K. Waltke, "1 Corinthians 11:2-16: An Interpretation," *Bibliotheca Sacra* 135 (January-March

1978):46-57; and Kenneth O. Gangel, "Biblical Feminism and Church Leadership," *Bibliotheca Sacra* 140 (January-March 1983):55-63.

21. This may be prejudicial on our part, of course. But some articles do not betray in print a suitable sense of *Angst* concerning the difficulties of the issues involved. They rather proceed along a point-by-point argument, much like a lawyer's brief, Q.E.D.

See, e.g., George W. Knight, III "The New Testament Teaching on the Role Relationship of Male and Female with Special Reference to the Teaching/Ruling Functions in the Church," *Journal of the Evangelical Theological Society* 18 (Spring 1975): 81-91; a tightly argued, thoroughly biblical presentation that seems to give no ground at all to issues raised by feminists. Carson, who himself appears to be a traditionalist, wonders whether Knight forces his issues by presuming that the first readers of 1 Corinthians 14:33b-38 had already read 1 Timothy 2:11-15. This would have been quite a feat, since none believes that the epistle to Timothy was written prior to the first epistle to Corinth. (D. A. Carson, *Exegetical Fallacies* [Grand Rapids: Baker Book House, 1984], 141.)

Or consider the approach of Thomas Howard who calls feminism "the most bitterly ruinous and the most grievously mendatious set of notions to appear on the public scene in a long time." ("A Traditionalist View," *Post American* 4 [May 1975]:10.) Not much discussion will follow this salvo!

22. Ellis speaks of "the great gulf which separates Paul's use of the OT from that of the rabbis." See E. Earle Ellis, *Paul's Use of the Old Testament* (reprint; Grand Rapids: Baker Book House, 1981), 74.

23. We agree with Osborne's conclusion on this difficult passage, "that the role functions of men and women are normative but that the cultural expression of that relationship in the wearing of veils is not. The cultural language of the passage and its contextual thrust both support this view." Grant Osborne, "Hermeneutics and Women in the Church," *Journal of the Evangelical Theological Society* 20 (December 1977):343.

24. Clark tells of a woman wearing a hat in a prayer meeting in her home; he wonders if she (or is the view her husband's?) feels constrained to wear a hat when she prays with her husband in bed at night. Gordon H. Clark, *1 Corinthians: A Contemporary Commentary* (Nutley, N.J.: Presbyterian & Reformed, 1975), 171.

While the wearing of a veil during public worship is an established practice for women in some religious communions (and may be validated by pursuing a survey of standard commentaries), the text is not really explicit that it must be a veil that covers the woman's head. The Greek word for veil (*kalumma*) is lacking in the text. The NIV margin reads "covering of [long] hair" in verses 4-7. It is at least plausible that the problem in the church of Corinth concerned the impropriety of women with shaven heads (perhaps former prostitutes) who were calling attention to themselves by taking prominent places in worship. Paul's concern for propriety took precedence over their concerns for participation.

25. William F. Orr and James Arthur Walther, *The Anchor Bible: 1 Corinthians* (Garden City, N.Y.: Doubleday & Company, 1976), 263.

26. Kari Torjesen Malcolm, *Women at the Crossroads: A Path Beyond Feminism and Traditionalism* (Downers Grove, Ill.: InterVarsity Press, 1982), 74-75.

27. A strong statement of the traditionalist position is given by Susan T. Foh, *Women and the Word of God: A Response to Biblical Feminism* (Grand Rapids: Baker Book House, 1980), 122-28. Her conclusion respecting the meaning of the difficult last verse of the section (1 Timothy 2:15) is an appeal to the genuine joys of motherhood for a woman who has faith in Christ. While this approach may be scorned by some feminists, it should not be dismissed. In reacting against traditional roles for women, there is a great danger of undervaluing the true biblical significance of mothering.

Perhaps the strongest defense of the traditionalist position on this text is presented by James B. Hurley, who believes that the instructions about women in 1 Timothy 2:11-12 are timeless and transcend any local or limited historical situation. See his, *Man and Woman in Biblical Perspective* (Grand Rapids: Zondervan Publishing House, 1981).

Those who see this passage as limited and related to a specific problem in the congregation at Ephesus include David M. Scholer, "Exegesis: 1 Timothy 2:8-15," *Daughters of Sarah* 1 (May 1975):7-8; and Mark Roberts, "Women Shall Be Saved: A Closer Look at 1 Timothy 2:15," *TSF Bulletin*, November-December 1981.

28. So Osborne, "Hermeneutics," 346.

29. Arguments based on rare words are precarious; arguments based on previously unrecognized meanings of rare words are disastrous. Nonetheless, we find at least intriguing the approach of Richard and Catherine Kroeger, "Ancient Heresies and a Strange Greek Verb," *Reformed Journal* (March 1979):12-14; "May Women Teach," *Reformed Journal* (October 1980):17, cited by Malcolm, *Women at the Crossroads*, 78-80. In the Kroeger's approach, the most difficult verse of the whole pericope (1 Timothy 2:15) is related to women who have given birth to illegitimate children through their pagan cultic experience, to whom Paul offers hope of salvation based on genuine faith, marked by continued holiness in life.

30. This is the conclusion of Osborne, "Hermeneutics," 347. We are impressed with his approach and are in agreement with his principal conclusions. It is also the conclusion of David M. Scholer: "In view of the evidence elsewhere in Paul . . . that women did, in fact, participate in the authoritative teaching and leadership ministry of the Church, it makes excellent sense to see 1 Timothy 2:11-12 as limited to this particular problem of heresy." ("Hermeneutical Gerrymandering: Hurley on Women and Authority," *TSF Bulletin* [May-June 1983], 13.)

31. See Foh's well-reasoned defense of traditional views, *Women and the Word of God*, 232-58. Calm, biblical reasons for change from traditional views are given by Richard and Joyce Boldrey, *Chauvinist or Feminist? Paul's View of Women* (Grand Rapids: Baker Book House, 1976).

Feminist theologians are doing the church a signal favor by causing us to reexamine the biblical imagery concerning God. Contrary to the assumptions of the old patriarchalism, it is evident that in the Bible God is not thought of exclusively in masculine terms. Patriarchal imagery is employed much more than feminine imagery, but both types of imagery are transcended, with neither being negated. The God of the Bible is neither "the Man Upstairs," nor "Mother Nature"; he is neither the Sky Father, nor the Earth Mother.

Donald G. Bloesch
Is the Bible Sexist?

Chapter 8

Balancing Our View of God

"Where am *I* in Scripture?"

It was in a class in her rabbinical seminary that Laura Geller suddenly realized how far removed was traditional religion from some major concerns of women. In one class in particular she was listening attentively to a fine lecture on Jewish blessings in daily life. The professor's point was that the steps of the life of faith are enwrapped in blessing. There are blessings for the man to say on rising in the morning, on hearing the voice of a child, on seeing a rainbow, on eating a meal. Enraptured with his own discourse, the professor said there are traditional blessings for every moment of life.

Not every moment.

Missing Blessing

It came to Geller that there were no traditional blessings for some of the very important moments in a woman's life. There was, for example, no blessing for a young woman on her first menstrual period. At first blush, one might dismiss the thought. Why should there be a blessing for her "curse"? But if we grant that a young woman's first period is a significant event in her life, why is there no appropriate blessing in a religion that offers blessings for seeing butterflies?

Wondering if she was right, Geller asked about her mother's first period, thinking perhaps there had been a blessing after all, and that it just had not been passed down to her generation.

Her mother told her, "When I had my first period, my mother slapped my face!" Geller, now very puzzled, went down the road and asked her grandmother why she had slapped her mother at that significant moment of her life.

The older lady said, "My dear, your mother looked pale. I was simply trying to help get color back to her face."

There was another reason, however, that remained unspoken: the slap was to avoid the influence of the "evil eye"—so much a part of Jewish folk religion.

Ceremonies for Women

Why was there a slap in the face for a young woman on a very important moment in her life, but blessings abounding for the young man at his every turning? There are ceremonies for the boy child on his circumcision, and on his becoming a member of the community. What are the ceremonies for a girl? When does a Jewish girl enter the community? What is her covenant ceremony? These are the kinds of things that have caused women of faith to reexamine the Bible as they explore their own meaning in our troubled day.

And when women turn to the Bible, they do not always get the solace and direction they need. They are beginning to ask, "Where am *I* in the Bible?"

Women and Abram

For example, Genesis 12:1-3 is one of the most significant portions of Torah regarding God's work in initiating his covenant with his people. This passage is foundational to the entire course of biblical theology. In a real sense, Genesis chapters 1-

11 are prologue; Genesis 12:1-3 is where the story of God and Israel begins.

But in these verses the focus is on Abram, not Sarai. When Abram responded in faith to Yahweh, he left the land of his birth, and "he took his wife Sarai, his nephew Lot, all the possessions they had . . . and they set out for the land of Canaan" (Genesis 12:5). How does a woman read this passage? Is she one of the things taken along? Where is her act of faith? Where is her identification? Does a woman have to identify with Abram in order to relate to that text?

Women at Sinai

Or think of Exodus 19, the chapter that sets the stage for the giving of the Decalogue, the central stipulations of the new covenant God made with Israel at Mount Sinai. Exodus 19 begins with language of grace and warning. God reminded Moses of all the wonders he had done for Israel, and then God told Moses to instruct the people how to prepare themselves for the reception of his new covenant:

> Now if you obey me fully and keep my covenant, then out of all nations you will be my treasured possession. Although the whole earth is mine, you will be for me a kingdom of priests and a holy nation (Exodus 19:5-6).

Would not the reader of these words expect that they speak to the whole nation, to all who were people of faith? The narrative continues. Instructions are given to ready the people for meeting God. They were not to set foot on the mountain before the specified time. In preparation for the third day they were to wash their clothes and not come near their wives, as they awaited the theophany of the Lord.

All of a sudden, the woman reader is taken aback. She might respond, "All of this is for *them*, not for me!" The words, "do not go near a woman" (Exodus 19:15, NASB) transform the

158   Finding the Biblical Balance

whole setting to an interaction between God and men, rather than between God and man.

It is this sort of thing that so troubles some women of faith that they are fearful of studying closely the biblical text, lest they turn away from it altogether.

Go to Yourself

Laura Geller promotes one solution for Jewish women. She takes a novel approach to a grammatical peculiarity of the language of God to Abram in Genesis 12:1. The Hebrew expression of the command, "get thee" (KJV), is an emphatic form that might be misunderstood by a beginning Hebrew student as "go to you."[1] Geller suggested that women may take this grammatical peculiarity as a mandate to "go to yourself." Since the Scriptures are not sufficiently directed to the needs of women, make of your own experience as a woman a new scripture, a new sacred text! Be creative in relating your own experience as a woman to develop a new canon of blessings and a new center of responses. Surely there is more that we can do for a young girl at a major moment of her life than to slap her face![2]

Evangelicals who hear these words may find themselves at such a distance from the traditional Jewish world that the lack of a blessing for a young woman on the beginning of her menses may not seem to be too important. But it *is* important, not only as an incident but as a symbol that women in traditional religion are sometimes regarded as onlookers rather than participants.

At the same time, the evangelical Christian (and the Orthodox Jew) will have difficulty in following the lead of hurting women by turning to themselves as a new sacred text. Our subjective experiences are not a fair exchange for the revelation of God in Scripture.

Go to the Text

Let's rather turn again to the sacred text we have and ask anew whether the distancing of women from the center of faith is a necessary part of Scripture, or perhaps is only a legacy from a male-oriented world that we may modify today.

For example, Exodus 19:15 may be translated in such a way as to include rather than exclude women. The New International Version nicely renders the verse: " 'Prepare yourselves for the third day. Abstain from sexual relations.' " Certainly, this is the intention of the Hebrew text. Women and men were to prepare themselves for the advent of God. It was not just for the men that Yahweh was about to descend to Mount Sinai: it was for the *people*.

The Nazirite Vow

Without turning in your Bible to the principal text, think for a moment about the Old Testament Nazirite vow. What were the three prohibitions? Do you remember? Ron has asked this question of seminary students. Invariably, there will be three prohibitions presented from memory:

> 1. No wine or anything remotely associated with the grape
> 2. No cutting of the hair
> 3. No sexual relations with a woman.

Class after class has given these responses. Only the first two are correct (Numbers 6:3-5). The text does *not* prohibit a man from sexual relations with a woman when he takes a Nazirite vow. The third prohibition concerns proximity to a dead person, even a beloved relative, during the time of the vow (Numbers 6:6-12, the longest section).

But here is the kicker: the Nazirite could be a woman! The text begins, "If a man or woman wants to make a special vow, a vow of separation to the LORD as a Nazirite, . . ." (Numbers 6:2). *A woman!*. Even when the text says "woman," we tend not to hear the word. That masculine pronouns are used in the remainder of the chapter helps to disguise the fact from us. But our negative attitudes toward women have excluded them from the vow; instead, have made them a part of the prohibitions of the vow.

Sexist Scriptures?

If we ask ourselves if the Scriptures are sexist, we may give a no-and-yes answer. The Bible was written principally by men and in a world in which the concerns and affairs of men were predominant. The Bible was written during a period of patriarchy. But these factors are not sufficient to declare the Bible sexist. In fact, it is with these factors in mind that the Bible has its great surprises!

Some Propositions

- The Hebrew Bible is interested in women from Genesis through Chronicles—the full extent of the Hebrew canon. In fact, in the patriarchal world of the Old Testament, it is instructive to find how often women play decisive roles. The highly contrasting books of Ruth (an alien woman coming to faith in Yahweh in a pastoral setting in the land) and Esther (a Jewish woman learning to demonstrate her faith in the harem of a pagan potentate) present godly women on center stage.
- The New Testament is even more interested in the place of women in the faith of the community. Here the public and private life of the Lord Jesus comes to bear in a dramatic fashion. Jesus affirmed women in numerous ways, sometimes in manners that shocked his male disciples. Christians need to imitate Christ not only in what he said, but in the way he behaved. Christians need also to see how Paul affirmed women in his actions. We are often so caught up in Paul's instructions for women to be silent, that we have ignored how prominent he regarded many very nonsilent women in the church (see Romans 16 where ten of the twenty-nine names Paul singles out for greetings—in a church he had not yet visited—are women coworkers in the gospel).[3]

- Women have even had a role in the composition of the Scripture. This is particularly true in the contributions of women to the psalmody of Israel, from the beautiful prayer of Hannah (1 Samuel 2:1-10) to the prophetic magnificat of Mary (Luke 1:46-55).[4]

- The Bible does not present women in universal sentimentality; the Bible is not a giant "Mother's Day Card." Women in the Bible can be exceedingly evil, greatly heroic, and rather ordinary—much like men.

- Negative portrayals of women in the Bible are usually balanced by positive ones, often in highly unexpected circumstances. Think, for example, of the story of Jezebel (beginning at 1 Kings 16:31)—perhaps the most wicked woman in the Bible. Her role is contrasted by a dramatically unexpected account of a woman's faith in Yahweh. This was the Phoenician widow of Zarephath who became the means of God's deliverance of his prophet Elijah during the years of drought in Israel (1 Kings 17:7-24).[5] As in the case of the Syrophoenician woman in the New Testament, whose faith so moved our Lord (Mark 7:24-30), the widow of Zarephath was a gentile committed to the God of reality.

- The Bible does place an emphasis on the role of motherhood for women—from Eve, who on the birth of Cain exulted at the work of Yahweh and perhaps thought she had given birth to the promised one himself (Genesis 4:1; cf. Genesis 3:15), to Blessed Mary, who did give birth to the child of promise (Luke 2:1-7). The Bible presents numerous stories of godly mothers in the Old Testament, and gives instructions for young mothers in the New. The words of Psalm 22:9-10 suggest that the first place a child may learn to trust in God is at its mother's breast. Even the apostle Paul likens himself to a mother in his deep affection for the believers at Thessalonica (1 Thessalonians 2:7; and as a father in verse ll). Those aspects of the women's movement that denigrate motherhood are not reflecting biblical perspectives.

- The Bible does not limit the role of women to motherhood nor does it insist that mothers may function only in their homes. The mothers of Israel and of the young church were able to function in a wide variety of areas beyond the home. We will speak of Miriam, Deborah, and Huldah at a later point in our book; the New Testament presents Lydia as the first Christian convert in Europe—a woman merchant who became a patron of the apostle Paul (Acts 16:13-15, 40).

- The Bible does present women as gifted for teaching ministries, particularly, but not exclusively, in the home. Both the Old Testament and the New Testament give examples of the teaching ministry of women in their homes. Proverbs speaks of the teaching of the mother along with that of the father (Proverbs 1:8). A mother cannot be an effective teacher of spiritual truth to her children unless she herself is taught. Timothy's mother Eunice and grandmother Lois are celebrated examples of the teaching ministry of women to children (and grandchildren) in the New Testament. Women of mature faith are encouraged to teach younger women in the New Testament (Titus 2:3-5).

- But women are also teachers of religious truth in the community at large. Think of the several prophets in the Old Testament who were women. Anna greeted and blessed the Christ child in the Temple (Luke 2:36-38). The New Testament also speaks of the four daughters of Philip who prophesied (Acts 21:9); it is inconceivable that they prophesied only to women.

- On some occasions women are the prime actors, the principal instigators, or the central foci of biblical narratives. These women are found in passages describing both reform and deliverance as well as rebellion and disaster.
- Some of the highest ideals of Hebrew spirituality and intellectual vitality are couched in feminine imagery. The most splendid example of this is the portrait of Lady Wisdom in Proverbs 1 through 9.[6]
- Perhaps most significantly, there are times God uses feminine imagery to describe himself. Among other things, this surprising aspect of revelation reminds us that God is Spirit, as Jesus taught the woman (!) at the well (John 4:24). To think of God the Father as a human male is an act of idolatry. God transcends the masculine and the feminine, yet he relates to his people in analogies of gender.[7] To the fatherless he is Father, to the motherless he is Mother, and to all he is Friend (Psalm 27:10).

The Bible and the Reader

In view of all these data, the fact that the Bible has been read as a sexist document says more about the reader and the cultural tradition that has influenced the reader than it does about the Bible itself. The male supremacists through time who have used the Bible to support their attitudes are matched today by radical feminists who find a male chauvinist behind every biblical bush.

If the Bible were truly sexist these positive affirmations of women would not be found. Note it well: These are not tokenisms or patronizing notices. These are not occasional pats on the collective heads of the little woman. The warp and woof of Scripture are imbued with a high sense of the dignity of women, even in the age of patriarchy. It appears that the factor of patriarchy in the Old Testament is a splendid backdrop for the presentation of the dignity, worth, ability, and gifting of women.

In the world in which we live, where women have the options of education, mobility, and access that men have, does it not make sense to encourage spiritually gifted women all the more to excel in the ministries of the gospel of Christ rather than to keep them veiled, silent, and suppressed?

It is the task of modern readers concerned about sexual equity to have a personal affirmative action program in their reading of the Bible. By this we do not mean the excess of changing every reference of God the Father to God the Mother. Rather we suggest that one emphasize those aspects of feminine virtue that the Bible does present but which we so often neglect.

Inclusive Language

Many evangelicals are alarmed about the recent publication of the inclusive language lectionary by the National Council of Churches.[8] The reasons for concern are significant, for the New Lectionary, based on the Revised Standard Version of the Bible, actually changes the wording of the Bible in an attempt to promote nonsexist attitudes among readers. In the process, phrases such as "God the Father" become "God the Father [*and Mother*]" (or sometimes "God"), "Lord" becomes "Sovereign," Jesus the "Son" of God becomes Jesus the "Child of God," "the Son of Man" becomes "the Human One," and the names of great women of the biblical period are inserted into the accounts where they had a role to play but were not actually named.

Here are some examples:

"Blessed be God the Father [*and Mother*] of our Sovereign Jesus Christ, . . ." (Ephesians 1:3).

"For God so loved the world that God gave God's only Child, that whoever believes in that Child should not perish but have eternal life" (John 3:16).

"But of that day and hour no one knows, not even the angels of heaven, nor the Child, but God only. As

were the days of Noah, so will be the coming of the
Human One" (Matthew 24:36-37).

"O house of Jacob, [*Rachel, and Leah*],
   come, let us walk in the light of God (Isaiah 2:5).

As we think over these passages, we find reason for concern. Does "God's only Child" really convey the sense of "his
one and only Son" (John 3:16)? Does "the Human One" fill
sufficiently the intention of "Son of Man" (Matthew 24:37)?
Perhaps. Perhaps not.

Metagesis

But what causes us serious concern are those places where
God is called "Mother." For this use of language does not draw
out something that is within the text, nor does it bring into the
text something from without. This is indeed a *changing* of the
text of Scripture. Perhaps the following familiar verse will demonstrate the enormity of what is involved:

For to us a child is born,
   to us an heir is given;
and the government will be on the shoulder of
   that one whose name will be called
"Wonderful Counselor, Mighty God,
   Everlasting Father [*and Mother*], Prince of Peace"
               (Isaiah 9:6).

In this example the prophetic name of Christ, which is intensely
significant, is deliberately changed to include the notion of
"Mother."

In the study of the Scriptures we speak of *exegesis* as the
"reading out" of the message of the Bible; that is, a presentation
of the intended teaching of the text. Mistakes in interpretation
are sometimes termed *eisegesis*, a "reading in" of things that are
not there but are thought to be there by the interpreter. But in the
new inclusive approach to Scripture we have what Ben
Patterson has described as *metagesis, a deliberate change of*

what the Bible does say. In this process the Bible is made a human tool for a current social agenda and not the revelation of God's will for our lives.

In a television interview one apologist of the New Lectionary defended the procedure in a most arrogant manner by saying: "The Bible belongs to the Church; not the Church to the Bible. The Church may make the Bible say whatever the Church wishes it to say."

Intentionality in Language

But the Bible is not a possession, it is revelation. The Bible is not a tool of the church, it is God's message to the church. The Bible is not ours to make it say what we want; it is to be heard and we are to listen and learn.

And what does the Bible say in this area? Scripture always speaks of God as Father; *never* in the text of Scripture is God called "our Mother." For those of us who believe in the intentionality of God in revelation, this choice of language has been made for us. We should not attempt to alter the facts to fit our (passing) tastes, no matter how pressing we believe the need to be.

Moreover, the issue is more important than is sometimes suspected. The Hebrew language, like German, Spanish, and French, has gender distinctions for its nouns. This means each common noun has an arbitrary gender marking; in most cases it is relatively easy to develop a feminine form for a masculine word or a masculine spelling for a feminine noun. In the Bible the words for God are *always* masculine—not sometimes, frequently, or usually—*always*, even when a goddess is clearly intended by the writer![9]

Bible and Counterculture

We believe this is because the Bible is counterculture. In an age in which the world of the imagination was filled with gods and goddesses who were ever fornicating, begetting, fighting, and dying—then came Torah which speaks in truth of Yahweh God.

Then came the Torah and soared aloft, as on eagles' wings, above all these notions. Not many gods but One God; not theogony, for a god has no family tree; not wars nor strife nor the clash of wills, but only One Will, which rules over everything, without the slightest let or hindrance; not a deity associated with nature and identified with it wholly or in part, but a God who stands absolutely above nature and outside of it, and nature and all its constituent elements, even the sun and all the other entities, be they never so exalted, are only His creatures made according to His will.[10]

It seems that the reluctance of the Bible to speak even of goddesses in the feminine was to avoid as strongly as possible the lapse of thinking of Yahweh as a goddess. Not because woman is inferior to man. Not because woman came after man. Not because of the bondage of patriarchy. But because of the ever present danger of slipping too quickly from goddess to nature religion, from revelation to imagination, from truth to error— and the loss of the eagles' wings of Torah.

Modern believers in the God of Scripture ought to be exceedingly cautious before they make the mistake the Bible refused to make. Speaking of God as Mother may sound chic. But it is a cheap chic that can cause one to slip; it is not worth the risk.

Feminine Imagery

On the other hand, the Bible does speak from time to time of God in *feminine imagery*. But the Bible does so in a way that keeps one from calling God goddess. This aspect of the Bible ought to be of great encouragement to women who continue to ask, "Where am *I* in the Bible?

One of the most striking areas of the feminine imagery of God is in Isaiah's description of the *maternal affection of Father God*. Isaiah does this both in overt imagery as well as in subtle words—words from which we may learn in wisdom.

Isaiah 54 uses the language of Yahweh as Husband to Israel whom he has made and redeemed, then rejected and regathered:

> For your Maker is your husband—
>> the LORD Almighty is his name—
> the Holy One of Israel is your Redeemer;
>> he is called the God of all the earth (Isaiah 54:5).

In the verses that follow Israel is called "a wife who married young,/only to be rejected" (v. 6), and her loving Husband says, "For a brief moment I abandoned you" (v. 7).

In these words the prophet uses imagery that will only work if God is the Husband and Israel the wife; to turn the terms around would destroy the thought, and to combine the elements would lead to a ludicrous situation: "For your Maker is your husband [*wife*]," and Israel is "a wife [*husband*] who married young." Such would lead only to laughter, not to the delicate beauty of this text.

Yet there is a subtlety in this text not evident in the translation. In the imagery of unquestioned masculine (God) to feminine (Israel) relationship, the prophet Isaiah uses subtle terms of feminine emotion as he describes the love of God:

> For a brief moment I abandoned you,
>> but with deep compassion I will bring you back
>>> (v. 7).

Womb Love

The word *compassion* in Hebrew is the word *raḥamîm*, an intensive plural noun related to the Hebrew term for womb (*reḥem/raḥam*). Intense compassion, for the Hebrew poet as for the modern reader, is often associated with the love of a mother for her young. The Bible uses both the noun and the verb forms of this word to describe God's intense love for his people.

The love of God the Father for his people is like unto the love of a woman for her own children, the offspring of her womb—with the necessary caveat: His love transcends even mother-love!

Can a mother forget the baby at her breast
  and have no compassion on the child she has
    borne?
Though she may forget,
  I will not forget you!
                (Isaiah 49:15).

Here the association of compassion with the womb is un-
mistakable. When God wishes to assure his people that he has
not forsaken nor forgotten them, he asks the rhetorical question
that might adorn any Mother's Day card: "Can a mother forget a
child borne of her womb, a baby who nursed at her breast?" The
answer we expect is, "Of course not!" The Bible is more realis-
tic. For, awful as it is even to imagine, there are mothers who
forget their children. But God's love surpasses even the love of
a woman for her child. His love is constrained by the wonder of
his character; it will not fail.

The Father's Compassion
So God speaks to his people as a Father who has the compassion of a mother for her child:

"But with everlasting loyal love
  I will have maternal compassion on you,"
says Yahweh your Redeemer
              (Isaiah 54:8, personal translation).

Though the mountains move and the hills shake, the loyal
love of Yahweh will not be shaken, nor will his covenant of
peace be removed, because of the enduring maternal affection
of our Father God (Isaiah 54:10).
God is Father—this is his own revelation. But God's love
transcends even that of a mother—this too is his revelation. It is
also our experience.[11]
We do not believe in metagesis; we take the Scriptures too
seriously for that. But we must also take the Scriptures seriously
enough that we learn to recapture the feminine imagery that has
been ignored for too long.

As a Hen

One of many examples of the feminine imagery of God found in the New Testament comes from the Savior Jesus in his touching lament over the sinfulness of Jerusalem:

> "O Jerusalem, Jerusalem, you who kill the prophets and stone those sent to you, how often I have longed to gather your children together, as a hen gathers her chicks under her wings, but you were not willing!" (Luke 13:34).

We have known these words from our youth, but it was only a few years ago that their full impact hit us. We live on a little farmlet and usually have a small flock of chickens among our animals. One day one of our three Aracaña hens was missing. These birds, believe it or not, lay eggs with shells of different pastel hues: green, blue, or pink. It was the "blue-egg" hen that was gone.

Some time later our missing hen was found parading across the front yard, followed by thirteen chicks! Since we had not scrubbed down the brooding room as yet, we brought the little chicks in to the utility room to keep them safe for the night and put the hen back in the chicken yard. Then, after scrubbing the brooding room carefully, we put the chicks on the fresh litter and went to bring their mother to them.

But which hen was the mother? All three looked about the same to us. We couldn't wait for a blue egg!

We put one hen at a time in with the chicks. The first two hens didn't even look at the chicks. They just pecked around a bit in the litter. Then we brought in the third hen.

It happened so fast we nearly missed it. It was as though she was a high-power vacuum cleaner and the chicks were so many particles of dust. With a flourish she had swept all thirteen under her wings—all of them!—and sat there daring anyone to try to take them away again.

To the rest of the chickens these chicks were competitors for food. Given the nature of chickens, the chicks might even have become munchies. But to their mother they were something else again.

When Jesus said of the city of Jerusalem, "how often I have longed to gather your children together, as a hen gathers her chicks under her wings," he was presenting a feminine image of himself. Only our urbanization keeps us from feeling the intense emotion and exquisite beauty of his words—words where Jesus the Son of God describes himself as Mother Hen.

Creative Reading

We need to learn to be creative readers, readers who recreate in our own imaginations the text of Scripture in a holistic manner. This process is based on the factor of the literary nature of much of Scripture. [12] In reading a literary piece the creative reader is attentive to the data and the nuances of the text. The creative reader is also concerned about conspicuous omissions.

Therefore it is proper in a study of the account of Abraham's near sacrifice of Isaac, for example, to ask about Sarah's possible feelings, actions, and responses. Isaac was her son also! Even when the text emphasizes the role of the father, there is a role played by the mother as well.

We find Joyce Landorf to be this kind of creative reader as she presents plausible constructions of the "hidden" lives of women in the Bible. Women often play unlikely roles in Scripture. One of the unexpected heroines was a gentile whore in Jericho who acted in faith in Yahweh and, at the risk of her own life, delivered the Jewish spies from the men of her town (Joshua 2; 6:25). Do we not wonder as we read this story what it was that might have led Rahab to become a prostitute? How did she come to faith in Yahweh? What motivated her to act so heroically against custom, nation, and all of our expectations? Landorf helps us flesh out this story by a disciplined use of creativity and imagination. [13]

We believe the New Testament gives us warrant for attempting to define more fully the spiritual dimensions in the lives of biblical women than one might have done based on the text of the Old Testament alone. A reading of Genesis, for example, will lead one to exclaim at the profound faith of Abraham. In fact, his faith is the paradigm for the faith of believers of all ages. "Abraham believed the LORD, and he credited it to him as righteousness" (Genesis 15:6; cf. Romans 4; Galatians 3:29).

Sarah's Faith

But Sarah was also a person of enormous faith. Like Abraham, her faith was sorely tempted when the promised birth of a son seemed to have been delayed intolerably. At one point she even laughed at the promise, then, in a very human way, lied about her laughter (Genesis 18:12-15). But when the child was born, the whole household was caught up with the new laughter of Sarah's joy:

> Sarah said, "God has brought me laughter, and
> everyone who hears about this will laugh with me."
> And she added, "Who would have said to Abraham
> that Sarah would nurse children? Yet I have borne
> him a son in his old age" (Genesis 21:6-7).

The point is this: While the focus of attention is on the role of Abraham, Sarah also has a role to play, a life to live, and a faith to demonstrate.

Our Mother

The modern city of Hebron is a place of recurring disputes between Jewish and Arab populations. Visitors are not always able to linger within the city or to visit the great mosque. This is a shame because that mosque is a shrine for all of us. It is built over the traditional site of the cave of Machpelah, which Abraham bought from Ephron the Hittite when Sarah died (Genesis 23). The marker on the memorial stone reads in Hebrew "Sarah our Mother." Indeed she is. Just as Abraham is our father in faith, so is Sarah our mother in faith. We are not only children of Abraham, we are the children of Sarah as well.

Daughters of Sarah

Is it possible that Peter's words concerning the faith of Sarah are intended to teach more than the subservience of a woman to her husband? Is there not also the sense of compliance and partnership in his faith? The true beauty of a woman is more than in adornments of beautifully coifed hair, exquisite jewelry, and stylish clothes. True beauty, Peter says,

> should be that of your inner self, the unfading beauty of a gentle and quiet spirit, which is of great worth in God's sight. For this is the way the holy women of the past who put their hope in God used to make themselves beautiful. They were submissive to their own husbands, like Sarah, who obeyed Abraham and called him her master. You are her daughters if you do what is right and do not give way to fear (1 Peter 3:4-6).

Certainly this text emphasizes the submission of a wife to her husband, as does Ephesians 5. But there is also within this text the concept of a woman's hope in God (v. 5), and her necessity to do right actions and not to fear (v. 6). Here, again, is the balance we sought to stress in the previous chapter. Moreover, Peter, like Paul, has words to the husbands:

> Husbands, in the same way be considerate as you live with your wives, and treat them with respect as the weaker partner and as heirs with you of the gracious gift of life, so that nothing will hinder your prayers (1 Peter 3:7).

Husbands are to be considerate of their wives, to respect them, and to respond to them as common heirs of life in faith together. The modifier "weaker" has often been used by people to demean women as being inferior in intellect, spirituality, or character. Such charges exist in the minds of bigots, not in the reality of women made in God's image. Women are weaker than men only in certain characteristics of physical strength. The husband is not to despise his wife for this general physical difference; rather, he is to show respect.

> Men are also to remember that women are coheirs of "the gracious gift of life." The sexual function and sexual distinctions are only for this age. Women will have an equal share in the new age; and even now in the life of the new age, they experience the grace of God equally with men (cf. Gal 3:27). Men must also remember that selfishness and egotism in the marriage relationship will mar their relationship with God.[14]

The Savior

It is in the Savior Jesus Christ that we have our finest instruction, example, and model of God's attitude toward women. Jesus' positive attitude toward women was probably never expressed better than by Dorothy Sayers:

> Perhaps it is no wonder that the women were first at the Cradle and last at the Cross. They had never known a man like this Man—there never has been such another. A prophet and teacher who never nagged at them, never flattered or coaxed or patronised; who never made arch jokes about them, never treated them either as "The women, God help us!" or "The ladies, God bless them!"; who rebuked without querulousness and praised without condescension; who took their questions and arguments seriously; who never mapped out their sphere for them, never urged them to be feminine or jeered at them for being female; who had no axe to grind and no uneasy male dignity to defend; who took them as he found them and was completely unself-conscious. There is no act, no sermon, no parable in the whole Gospel that borrows its pungency from female perversity; nobody could possibly guess from the words and deeds

of Jesus that there was anything "funny" about woman's nature.[15]

When rabbinical student Laura Geller began to wonder where she as a woman might learn to identify herself in Scripture, she decided too early that the identification cannot be made. In her frustration, she turned to herself as a new sacred scripture. Had she decided to stay with the text of the Bible, she might have discovered considerably more in the text for a woman's identification than one might first think.

The Christian woman has a distinct advantage over the Jewish reader of the Bible. She has Christ. In Christ she finds new meaning for herself as a woman, for in him she discovers dignity she has never known before.

In Christ she knows God, and she learns that her new sense of dignity is no aberration. The incarnation makes God known, it explains the Father to us all (John 1:18). As Jesus accords dignity to women, he does so as an act of explaining the heart of God to her.

No wonder women were first at the Cradle and last at the Cross. No wonder women were first at the empty Tomb as well.

Have you as a woman ever asked, Where am I in the Bible? Stick close to the Savior Jesus, and you'll find out.

Chapter 8, Notes

1. The words are made of the imperative form of the verb "go" and a preposition with a pronominal suffix. Grammarians call this construction a dative of personal reference. The point of the construction is that the command is not one that can be delegated, it must be done by the one commanded: *You* go!" This construction cannot be translated readily into English. The NIV says merely "leave . . . and go."

2. This account was given by Rabbi Laura Geller in her keynote address at the conference, "The Emerging Jewish Woman," 28 October 1984, Portland, Oregon.

3. This is a point made by Reta Finger, "Paul: A Woman's Ally," *The Other Side*, August 1983, 19-20. Further, comments about Euodia and Syntyche often are limited to the observation that they did not get along (hardly an exclusively feminine trait—given the history of controversy in the church!), and

not to the fact that they are called by Paul, "women who have contended at my side in the cause of the gospel" (Philippians 4:3)—hardly language appropriate for "silent learners" only.

4. Arguments that Priscilla may have been a writer or a cowriter of the book of Hebrews continue to surface. For our part, this is a suggestion that has at least as much merit as the continuing assertion of some that the book was written by Paul. The idea was first presented in modern times by Adolf von Harnock; a recent development is given by Ruth Hoppin, *Priscilla: Author of the Epistle to the Hebrews* (New York: Exposition Press, 1969).

5. See Ronald B. Allen, "Elijah the Broken Prophet," *Journal of the Evangelical Society* 22 (1979): 193-202.

6. A theme developed at length in Ronald B. Allen, *The Majesty of Man: The Dignity of Being Human* (Portland, Ore.: Multnomah Press, 1984), 153-70.

7. A point developed with balance by Donald G. Bloesch, *Is the Bible Sexist?: Beyond Feminism and Patriarchalism* (Westchester, Ill.: Crossway Books, 1982), 67. Many helpful and insightful ideas of the feminine imagery of God in the Bible are presented by Virginia Ramey Mollenkott, *The Divine Feminine: The Biblical Imagery of God as Female* (New York: Crossroad, 1984). However, in our opinion, Mollenkott vitiates her point of view by her enthusiastic embrace of sentiments of women such as Dame Julian of Norwich, who speaks of "Mother Jesus" (p. 30), and concludes, "God rejoices that he is our Mother" (p. 119).

8. Three are planned. The first is, *An Inclusive Language Lectionary: Readings for Year A* (Atlanta: John Knox Press; New York: The Pilgrim Press; Philadelphia: The Westminster Press, 1983). Some in free evangelical churches are not familiar with the lectionary format. A lectionary is a listing of readings from various portions of the Bible (Old Testament, Epistles, and Gospels), which are used in the public readings of the church at worship. These readings are tied in to the church year. Some have attacked the new lectionary on the wrong flank. The concept of having a pattern of selected readings of the Bible that is used by churches in common throughout the world has ancient roots and can be very constructive in the worship experience. What is "new" is the inclusive language, not the concept of the readings.

Further, we should observe that there is another new lectionary that has not received the amount of publicity as the one produced by the National Council of Churches. This is *Hearing the Word*, produced by the people of St. Stephen and the Incarnation Episcopal Church in Washington, D.C. *Hearing the Word*, which uses various Bible translations rather than just the RSV, is reviewed by Mark Olson in *The Other Side*, March 1984, 34.

9. See, for example, 1 Kings 11:33 where the goddess Ashtoreth is designated in the Hebrew text by the masculine *god*.

10. U. Cassuto, *A Commentary on the Book of Genesis, Part I: From Adam to Noah*, trans. Israel Abrahams (Jerusalem: The Magnes Press, The Hebrew University, 1961), 8.

Some false trails have been followed by enthusiasts for God as feminine. My colleague Ralph Alexander reports he heard a woman enthusiast at a Society of Biblical Literature meeting say that the word for God *'elohim* is a feminine plural. It is in fact a masculine plural. The worst thing about that remark was that not enough people in the audience laughed—such is the state of Hebrew studies in our day.

There have also been those who have said that the name Jesus (Y'shua) in Hebrew is a feminine name! Richard Wurmbrand declares that when Joseph was told he was to name the child of Mary "Jesus," it was "as though we were to call a boy Helen or Katherine. A Man with a female name. It was this mystery which was expressed in the outward appearance of an Orthodox priest: he had to have a beard but wear a woman's robe." *Stronger Than Prison Walls* (New Jersey: Fleming Revell, 1969), 33-34; cited by Margaret Wold, *The Shalom Woman* (Minneapolis: Augsburg Publishing House, 1975), 37. It is difficult to know who or what is given the greater affront in this ludicrous remark, Orthodox priests or language itself. Wurmbrand suffered terribly in a communist prison cell for fourteen years, and we honor him for his faith in God. We cannot understand, however, his blunder concerning the gender of the name of our Lord. Perhaps he has confused the sound of the ending of the word with the feminine termination—the sound is similar, but the spelling is different. The difference is between a consonantal *Ayin* and a *He* used as a vowel marker. Yet certainly, even if one might make such a mistake, would he or she not wonder why this "strange" name was not commented upon by someone earlier in the history of the church? Even by Joseph himself?

11. Some of this section is based on Ronald B. Allen, "The Father's Compassion," *The Bible Newsletter*, May 1984, 3.

12. See Leland Ryken, *How to Read the Bible as Literature* (Grand Rapids: Zondervan Publishing House, 1984).

13. Joyce Landorf, *He Began with Eve* (Waco, Tex.: Word Books, 1983), 61-90. In addition to Eve and Rahab, Landorf presents short stories of the lives of Jochebed, Abigail, and Bathsheba. There are many good fictionalized studies of women in the Bible. A very popular one is Gien Karssen, *Her Name Is Woman* 2 volumes (Colorado Springs, Colo.: NavPress, 1975, 1977).

14. Edwin A. Blume, "1 Peter," in *The Expositor's Bible Commentary*, ed. Frank E. Gaebelein, (Grand Rapids: Zondervan Publishing House, 1981), 12:237. Moreover, it is possible that the phrase "be considerate as you live with your wives," has to do not just with general living together but with sexual life together as well.

15. Dorothy L. Sayers, *Are Women Human?* (Grand Rapids: Wm. B. Eerdmans Publishing Co., 1971), 47.

A wife of noble character who can find?
She is worth far more than rubies.
Her husband has full confidence in her
and lacks nothing of value.
She brings him good, not harm,
all the days of her life.

. . . .

Charm is deceptive, and beauty is fleeting;
but a woman who fears the LORD is to be praised.
Give her the reward she has earned,
and let her works bring her praise at the city gate.
Proverbs 31:10-12, 30-31

Chapter 9

Biblical Nobility

Some women shudder when they hear the "Proverbs 31 Lady" mentioned. They feel she has been used to thump them on Mother's Day too often. One woman has told us, "If I hear one more time about 'hands and flax' [v. 13] as the epitome of being a woman, I'll scream!"

It is unfortunate but some women have been led to believe that if they do not measure up in every respect to the model of Proverbs 31, they are failures as wives and mothers, inadequate as women, and undeserving of God's blessing. The chapter is too often held up as an impossible model to emulate.

Yet the chapter must continue to have its appeal, for we are aware of three recent books on it. Two of them are devotional encouragements to *be* the Lady of Proverbs 31. Perhaps more women will respond to the sentiment of the third book: *The Proverbs 31 Lady, And Other Impossible Dreams.*[1]

Ruby

Gospel singer Cynthia Clawson echoes the modern lament of countless women in her haunting song, "Ruby." The song presents the story of a woman who desperately wants to be a Proverbs 31 woman. This is seen in the refrain:

Lord, I want to be a ruby for you,
> and feel your pleasure in all I do.
But I need your help
> for this weary way,
> 'cause I don't feel
> I can be
> superwoman one more day.[2]

In her desire to feel the Lord's pleasure upon her, Ruby has
given up her aspiring career as an actress to play all the expected
roles in the home for her husband, her children, and her neighbors. To her husband she is a siren, a clone of Cleopatra. She
meets her childrens' every need, a Florence Nightingale incarnate. She is always there for her neighbors as well, playing
every role they demand.

But time goes by for Ruby. Her husband has tired of the
role she has played and has left her for a new enchantress. Her
children are all grown now; they no longer need her either. Now
all alone, there is one thing at least she can do. She can act on a
local stage. But her neighbors who come to see her perform are
impressed only with her wrinkles; poor Ruby is starting to show
her age.

And at night all alone as she climbs up the stairs,
She remembers her prayer:
Lord, I want to be a ruby for you!

But Ruby cannot be a superwoman any longer.

Down with Superwoman!

We propose that Proverbs 31 should not be regarded as an
impossible model for the believing woman of this or any age.
Instead of seeing this chapter as a template for *a woman*, and
then judging one another's deficiencies on the basis of its exact-
ing requirements, let's see in this beautiful poem the many dimensions of *Woman*. That is, in Proverbs 31 we have a presentation of all the kinds of things women *may do* rather than an im-
position on what a given woman *must do* to feel God's pleasure.

This chapter is a cross-section of women rather than a picture of Superwoman.

Not only are Christian women no longer desiring the Superwoman image, secular feminists are also turning their backs on unrealistic demands for women. It is true some women seem to have unlimited resources of energy and ability, and are able to juggle three lives in their one person. But most women are not able to go at such a pace for very long any more than most men.

Betty Friedan said in a lecture in New York at the end of the seventies, "We told our daughters you can have it all. Well, can they have it all? Only by being a Superwoman. Well, I say *no* to Superwoman!"[3]

Ellen Goodman comments further on the Superwoman concept:

> The Superwoman myth is exploding like an over-stuffed sofa. Women are no longer willing to look inside themselves for all the answers and all the energy. At the turn of the decade, they don't want a Superwoman pep talk anymore. They long for something more precious and more realistic: a support system—of families, the workplace and the community—to fend off this cultural kryptonite.[4]

The lesson secular feminists are learning needs also to be learned by the Christian woman: Not only is it not possible to be a Superwoman, it is not necessary to be one. The "Proverbs 31 Lady"—so often used as a scriptural mandate to be all things to all people at all times—needs to be seen in a new perspective. Proverbs 31 is far more wonderful than most people realize.

The Lady and Wisdom

The exquisite poem of Proverbs 31:10-31 is the climax of the biblical wisdom tradition given in the Book of Proverbs. It is not an ornamental addendum, as some editions of the Bible might suggest. Nor is this poem a part of the wisdom of King Lemuel's mother (Proverbs 31:1-9), as is often supposed.

Proverbs 31:10-31 is a distinct unit. It is a highly artistic poem in the form of an acrostic, the first word of each verse beginning with a letter in sequence in the Hebrew alphabet. The poem is anonymous. It serves as the Epilogue to the book, the grand coda to the whole piece, and has as important a place to play in the book's structure as does the Prologue (Proverbs 1:1-7).

The structure of the Book of Proverbs is more complex than many readers realize, but there is an overarching unity to the book that transcends its complexity. Just as the prologue prepares us for the content of the book and leads us into them, so the epilogue is a reflection of the basic themes and a recapitulation of the book.

The Book of Proverbs often seems to be addressed to the training of a young man in the ways of wisdom (e.g., Proverbs 1:8, 10, 15; 2:1; 3:1; etc.). But most surprisingly the book concludes with a portrait of a mature woman who embodies the ideals of wisdom itself! This portrayal of the wise woman presents one of the strongest biblical passages on the dignity, worth, and full humanity so many women of faith long to realize today. But, instead of seeing this chapter as the best word of God on true liberation, many women see in it a new bondage. The last chapter of Proverbs ought to be regarded as one of God's happy messages in the Bible, not as new fetters for an overworked and busy woman.

A Woman of Valor

The description of the woman in Proverbs 31:10 as a wife "of noble character" reflects a term used elsewhere in the Old Testament to signify people of exceptional valor, ability, efficiency, or moral worth. The question format of this verse, "A wife of noble character who can find?" does not mean this type of woman doesn't exist. Rather the descriptive phrases that follow in this beautiful acrostic poem show what women can be and can do in the home and in the community, and in the process how they can be truly fulfilled in the context of God's blessing.

Her Husband

We were once in a group where Proverbs 31 was being discussed. One of the women pointed to the words of verse 13 that speak of the industry of the woman ("and works with eager hands") and contrasted them with the words in verse 23 describing the husband ("at the city gate,/where he takes his seat.") She concluded that this passage must have been written by a man who wished to keep his wife busy so that he could enjoy the good life.

She compared these verses to her own experience at family gatherings where the women's hands were exceedingly busy with meal and dishes, and the husbands said "nice job" as they went down the hall to watch the football game. Holiday times can be described in this way for countless families.

This is neither the intention nor the teaching of Proverbs 31. The husband, to whom the passage refers in passing, is not watching the Cowboys play the Redskins when he sits with the men at the gate of the city. He is one of the town elders taking his place in a seat of honor to adjudicate problems of the community. The point of the verse is that he is able to do his work so well because he finds his wife's work to be a complement to his own; he is not at all threatened by her many interests and aggressive activities. He is fulfilled in his work and she is fulfilled in hers, and they have a sense of mutuality and respect for each other.

Her Work

Women, Proverbs 31 projects, have many options for combining work in the home and outside the home, work for material gain with work that is voluntary and charitable. Here are some of the phrases:

She cares for the needs of her family:
- She provides food for her family (vv. 14-15)
- She sees that all are clothed well (v. 21)
- She watches the affairs of the home (v. 27)

- She is a credit to her husband (v. 11)
- She is a joy to her children (v. 28).

She is a manager and an entrepreneur:
- She directs her servants (v. 15)
- She buys fields and plants vineyards with her own money (v. 16)
- She is engaged in commerce (v. 18)
- She has a small business (v. 24).

She is an artisan and craftsperson:
- She works with wool and flax (vv. 13, 19)
- She makes garments and coverings (vv. 22, 24).

She is industrious:
- She rises early or works late (vv. 15, 18)
- She works hard at her tasks (v. 17)
- She is not lazy (v. 27).

She is balanced:
- She meets the needs of the poor (v. 20)
- She cares for herself as well (v. 22).

The text puts all these items together, not to make impossible demands upon all women, but that we may see the options that are open to women. What may women do? Women are given no limitations in this text, only options and open doors.

Her Options

The noble woman of Proverbs 31 is a woman who has options before her for personal growth,

> She is clothed with strength and dignity;
>> she can laugh at the days to come (v. 25);

for intellectual stimulation,

> She speaks with wisdom,
>> and faithful instruction is on her tongue (v. 26);

for family satisfaction,

> She watches over the affairs of her household
>   and does not eat the bread of idleness (v. 27);

and for community affairs,

> She opens her arms to the poor
>   and extends her hands to the needy (v. 20).

Furthermore, she is the epitome of biblical piety,

> Charm is deceptive, and beauty is fleeting;
>   but a woman who fears the LORD is to be praised
>   (v. 30).

Her Piety

When the writer speaks of this woman's fear of Yahweh, the heart of Proverbs and the core of biblical wisdom have come to the fore. Proverbs 1:7 points the way to what biblical wisdom is all about:

> The fear of the LORD is the beginning of knowledge,
>   but fools despise wisdom and discipline.

Here at the end of the book it is a woman who has reached the goal and shown the way for us all. Given the prominent role of Lady Wisdom in Proverbs 1 through 9,[5] this should come as no surprise.

Her Liberation

Numerous passages in the Bible, especially in the Mosaic Covenant, may be regarded by us today—and perhaps were even then—as limiting a woman's potential for growth and personhood to the role of wife and mother. We do not deny that these factors were a part of Israel's experience in the Old Testament period. It is, however, against the backdrop of this patriarchy that the challenge of Proverbs 31 takes on such great importance.

Within a world dominated by men, there was still the possibility—surely, even the divine expectation—that women might achieve in life the full outworking of the gifts and abilities God had given them. Read in this way, Proverbs 31 is truly a revolutionary chapter. *This* is the Magna Charta for biblical women in the Hebrew Scriptures.

A Personal Balance

As women read these words today they will be prompted to find a biblical and personal balance between the demands of their homes and their careers, their communities and their persons. God's desires for a woman may be seen to be expansive, not restrictive, in such a passage. Moreover, women will find in all their activities opportunities to display genuine piety, the source of beauty that is genuine and nonfading.

A woman of biblical faith has good reasons for finding a strong sense of worth in the home and family. Career women should not look down upon those who find fulfillment in the home. Certainly the woman of Proverbs 31 has her center in the home.

But women who are content with home and family should not look down upon others who attempt to balance home and career. For the woman of Proverbs 31 was balancing both nearly three thousand years ago, with the blessing of husband, children, community—and the smile of the Lord!

One of the benefits of the women's movement has been to give the modern wife and mother the options idealized in Proverbs 31 for a wife to have her own bank account, her own credit history, and to make major purchases in her own name.[6] In no sense should these abilities threaten or imperil a woman's oneness with her husband, for he finds his own sense of personal worth enhanced with such an astute wife. And she on her part may have more sense of worth and dignity to contribute to their marriage relationship.

Their Arms—Together!

It was estimated on a recent "60 Minutes" broadcast that over half of all mothers of young children in the United States work outside the home. As Christian parents, we have opportunities today to share together in new and creative ways the loving nurture of our children and the responsibilities of home. We certainly cannot expect the wife and mother to do everything at home in addition to her job; the husband has to do more than just "sit at the gate."

In our own experience we have been growing over the years into more of a partnership in these areas. A husband's growing involvement with his wife in the work at home may be a major element in their growing together as a couple.

Our marriage began as many must have in the sixties. We have a wall plaque someone gave us that tells the story: "It begins when you sink in his arms and ends with your arms in the sink!" But things change. Some jobs we share, some we have as our own—but we share in the work around the house today much more than when we were first married.

What is true of our care for the home is also true of our parenting. Our mutual parenting has been strengthened by the fact that we both work outside the home. Instead of being a detriment to the family, the mother's work outside the home may be a distinct advantage in that the father may, of necessity, be brought more fully into the parenting process.

Widening Her World

Another advantage that may come from the wife working outside the home is her increased world view. Our lives are very much involved with our children, of course. But wholesome Christian living is more than simply living for the children. By the fact that Bev has worked outside the home, she has things to share with the family about her workday, her relationships with people, her opportunities for witnessing to her faith in Christ, and her continual process of personal development.

Three-Feet Tall

These are things some housewives never get to enjoy. The complaint of many suburban housewives is that all day long they have no one to talk to who is over three-feet tall. When we talk over our day, we are able to share with each other on a mutual level of stimulation on subjects relating both to our jobs as well as to the home and family.

We do not believe the "no one to talk to over three-feet tall" syndrome should continue, even among full-time housewives. Certainly, there are abundant opportunities these days for mothers of small children to interact with other adults on significant levels during the course of the week. But many women do not take advantage of these opportunities and the only things they are able to add to the dinner conversation are such husband-pleasing topics as how many diapers Johnny went through or what a good buy she got on the lettuce at the store that morning.

Now hear us out: diapers and groceries are the stuff of life when you have small children. A wife *should* be able to talk to her husband about these things, for they are significant. But she needs as well to have an adequate interaction with peers that relates to other areas of living. A woman needs intellectual, spiritual, and emotional stimulation just as a man does. The woman of Proverbs 31 did more than change diapers and grapple with groceries. Her works brought her praise at the city gate (v. 31).

The husband who complains that his wife is dull and not at all like the women who interact with him about important things at work, may have himself to blame for not helping her find the creative, stimulating, and interactive aspects of her life that we all need.

Women and the Word

A good starting point is a women's Bible study class. The principal aim of these classes, of course, is the development of true spirituality based upon sound biblical instruction. But at least as important as the spiritual dimension is the tremendous opportunity these groups provide for serious interaction with caring adults. We highly commend such organizations as Women's Bible Study Fellowship and Community Bible

Studies, as well as classes for women sponsored by local churches, for what they do to improve the sense of wholeness for the Christian woman.[7]

Back to School

Other areas open to housewives today are classes in their local community college. These classes can be taken in the evenings as well as during times when the children are in school. A loving thing a husband can do for his wife during the years that they have small children is to take care of the children himself one evening a week and make it possible for her to take a special interest course at the community college. If he is not yet up to cooking the evening meal, one night a week of fast food will probably not destroy family nutrition forever.

How sad it is to come across Christian families where an autocratic husband forbids his wife to attend even a women's Bible class. We know of some families where this is done on the husband's greatly mistaken impression that his wife's involvement in the class will take away necessary time from her work at home. These husbands have only themselves to blame if dinner conversation cannot go beyond diapers and groceries.

Work and Aggression

But working outside the home can also be a problem for the woman—a major problem. She may strike out in aggression against male exploitation and imitate the very men about whom she has such rage.

> The determined tough-faced women who pursue what has been labeled a "macho-feminist" course appear to be buying into the male culture they found so offensive in men and are setting aside their womanhood. Ironically, as they struggle to define themselves, they are mimicking the men they resent.[8]

But this is not the picture of woman at work as developed by Proverbs 31. That woman is not imitating men at all. She is happy and secure in her own identity as a woman. Furthermore, her husband and children are delighted in her identity as a wife, mother, and business woman. They take pride not only in her knitting but also her business deals!

The Proverbs 31 woman is balanced. She is mother and wife. She is craftsperson and businesswoman. She is homemaker and philanthropist. She is manager and God-fearer. She is woman. She does not stress her professional career advancement to the detriment of her family and children. She does not reach for reform of business and government and lose her own spirituality or sensitivity in the process. Unfortunately, as Jepsen has noted, this balance is not often found in today's career woman:

> Some good things have happened because of the women's movement; I would be the last to deny that. Changes have been made that were long overdue. But in the process we have lost sight of some very important aspects of life also. The movement has focused so much upon professional career advancement, education, and governmental reforms that the role model for women that emerges from the rhetoric is still fragmented. Only one aspect of women's identity has been focused upon. The sensitive and spiritual side which is an area of great strength and gift in women, has been all but ignored by many.[9]

Enhance Life

It is in the area of spiritual strength and sensitivity that Christian women must have their voices heard in the current debate. This biblical balance is necessary for the women's movement to truly enhance life rather than just complicate it. Lynda Johnson Robb writes of the need for Christian women to speak out for these balancing areas. She says the changes women are seeking are more than political, educational, and governmental. They are "life-enhancing, family-enhancing and spirit-enhancing."[10]

Just a Housewife

There are several problems with the expression, "just a housewife." As has long been observed, being a housewife and mother can be a demanding, productive, and fully satisfying life. This is no little feat! Further, many women who are just housewives do numerous things beyond the boundaries of the home.

For example, a pastor's wife might not be employed outside the home. But depending upon her gifts, interests, and abilities, she may be immensely involved in her husband's ministry. We know of some pastors' wives who have physical illness or other reasons that inhibit them from an active role in their husbands' ministries. But we also know many pastors' wives whose unofficial, unpaid job description boggles the mind.[11]

Volunteers

Many women who are "just housewives" are engaged in significant volunteer activities for church, school, and community. The benefit these women provide in public service is incalculable; in fact, that is one of the problems. We do not fully realize how much valuable work these women do. When they later try to enter the work force, they find it difficult to present the record of their unpaid volunteer labor as a convincing factor in their resumes.

We are very much in favor of a practice that has been initiated at our public school. There, volunteers sign in and out on special time cards. This serves two important purposes. For one thing, the principal of the school now has an objective evaluation of the amount of time contributed by volunteer workers. This is a major element in presenting the reasonableness of district budgeting requests; money is being saved in many areas by unpaid volunteer labor. In addition, the volunteer worker who wishes later to enter the work force is able to present an objective evaluation of her work as a volunteer. She may say to a prospective employer, "I have logged 650 hours of work as a volunteer at my public school. Here is my work record and my principal's evaluation."

Women in Patriarchy

But in all of these things we still must return to the Scriptures and ask if we are thinking rightly in advocating for some women of faith the possibility of expanding their roles of influence beyond the home.

Let's consider again the factor of the patriarchy. Under the strong Hebrew patriarchy that existed for much of the biblical period, it was assumed that a woman's only place was in the home. But we err if we equate the experience "in the home" for a woman in ancient Israel with that of a modern suburban housewife. In a largely agrarian economy, the household was a place where the woman was heavily involved in the whole process of food production and management.[12]

Modern culture has done more to take the man out of the home, breaking the sense of working together that existed under patriarchy, than to strengthen the woman's sense of well-being. Furthermore, under patriarchy the husband had an intense role in the raising and nurturing of children. In many modern families the father has hardly any part in the life of the young child.

Our point is this: An immense cultural gap exists between family life in the biblical world and family life today that cannot be bridged easily by the rubric, "a woman's place is in the home."

There are many indications, even in the patriarchy of biblical culture, that women were able to take strong and vigorous positions of leadership within the home, the cult, and the community. This does not mean women had access to all positions of leadership. But there are surprising instances of strong and able women in significant leadership roles in the men's world of ancient Israel.

Miriam

Think of Miriam, sister of Moses and Aaron. Her role in leading the formative nation Israel through the forty years in the desert was exceeded only by her two brothers. Our notice of this is often overshadowed by the account of her animosity toward Moses during one difficult period of their relationship.

Numbers 12 describes the attack on Moses instigated by Miriam and joined by Aaron. This attack resulted in the divine outbreak of temporary skin disease on Miriam. While she and her brother Aaron were guilty of foolish and rebellious sin in speaking against Moses (Numbers 12:11), the story only works on the premise that Miriam was truly a potential rival to Moses for the leadership of the nation.

Deborah

A positive illustration of a woman's prominent national leadership is the dramatic story of Deborah the prophetess and judge (Judges 4 and 5). With Deborah we find many biblical conventions convoluted.

Often we read in the Bible about a significant man and find only a parenthetical mention of the name of his wife. With Deborah the situation is quite reversed: Her husband's name would only be known by a true champion of Bible trivia (Lappidoth, Judges 4:4).

Deborah's role is sometimes minimized by male commentators as occasioned only by the lack of adequate male leadership. It is said that had Barak, the leader of the army, been a stronger man, Deborah would have been a more reserved woman, occupied at home. Perhaps she might have helped make Lappidoth famous.

But these are imported values. This is what the text says:

Deborah, a prophetess, the wife of Lappidoth,
was leading Israel at that time. She held court under
the Palm of Deborah between Ramah and Bethel in
the hill country of Ephraim, and the Israelites came

to her to have their disputes decided. She sent for
Barak son of Abinoam from Kedesh in Naphtali and
said to him, "The LORD, the God of Israel, com-
mands you: 'Go, take with you ten thousand men of
Naphtali and Zebulun and lead the way to Mount
Tabor. I will lure Sisera, the commander of Jabin's
army, with his chariots and his troops to the Kishon
River and give him into your hands'" (Judges 4:4-7).

Deborah's leadership of the nation is noted by the biblical
historian without prejudice or embarrassment. She is so significant that she may be compared to the later judge Samuel who
also "sits in court" in auspicious places to settle disputes by the
word of the Lord (1 Samuel 7:15-17). When Deborah speaks to
Barak it is with a sure word of Yahweh, just as when Samuel
speaks to David. Barak's trust in her and dependence on her is
so excessive that he agrees to obey the word of the Lord through
her only with the concession that she join him on the battle
march. Deborah's words to Barak state the case well:

"Very well," Deborah said, "I will go with you.
But because of the way you are going about this, the
honor will not be yours, for the LORD will hand
Sisera over to a woman." So Deborah went with
Barak to Kedesh (Judges 4:9).

Barak's weakness did allow the glory of the battle to go to
a woman under the most unethical of circumstances. Jael, the
unlikely heroine—whose husband, Heber, is also little known—
put the enemy Sisera to death in one of the most outrageous
breaches of desert hospitality to be found in ancient literature
(4:17-22).

Barak was a weak man, and he lost the glory of the defeat
of the enemy to a housewife. But Barak's weakness was not the
reason for Deborah's leadership. Her gifting and leadership
were from the Lord, and preceded Barak's dubious acts of valor.

No numbers game may help us escape the implications of
the story of Deborah. It does not matter that she is the only

woman judge of Israel in the period between the death of Joshua and the coronation of Saul. That a woman of impeccable character and unquestioned gifting of God could be the major political and religious leader of Israel during the period of patriarchy, should put to rest the approach of some traditionalists that a woman cannot be blessed by God in a leadership role outside the home. Further, the fact that she was a married women, and likely a mother, is a part of the picture. Here is a biblical heroine whose life had more to it than dishes and diapers. Her mouth spoke the word of Yahweh!

Huldah

The story of Huldah is another example. This great prophetess was associated with the high priest Hilkiah and king Josiah in bringing about the spiritual renewal in the latter days of the kingdom of Judah. The story of Josiah's reforms, beginning in 621 B.C., is well-known by readers of the Hebrew Scriptures. It was the last gasp of true spirituality before the southern kingdom slid to ignominy and disaster under the Babylonian siege and destruction of Jerusalem, culminating in 586 B.C.

One of the least known aspects of the reform of Josiah is the role taken by Huldah the prophetess of Yahweh. When Hilkiah the priest discovered the long-forgotten Book of the Law in the inner recesses of the temple, he gave it to Shaphan the secretary who in turn informed Josiah of the remarkable find. The young king, only twenty-six years old at the time, responded to the reading of the Book of the Law with repentance and remorse. Then he sent his principal attendants along with Hilkiah the priest to find a new word from Yahweh to mark this great discovery. To whom did Hilkiah and his august entourage go? To a woman!

> Hilkiah and those the king had sent with him went to speak to the prophetess Huldah, who was the wife of Shallum son of Tokhath, the son of Hasrah, keeper of the wardrobe. She lived in Jerusalem, in the Second District (2 Chronicles 34:22; 2 Kings 22:14).

Why did they go to her? Was it not because king, priest, and administrators all recognized that in her would be found the true word of Yahweh? Here is the amazing thing: There were other prophets who were also true spokespersons for Yahweh at the time. These included even the great Jeremiah and his contemporary Zephaniah—both writing prophets! It is not that there was no man to whom these leaders might go so they had to settle for a woman. God led them to her because God had given to her the words he wished them to hear.

When contemporary traditionalists say that women may not have leadership roles in church or society unless we dismiss all the biblical data, it appears that not *all* the data need be turned upside down. Some biblical texts speak quite clearly of women in significant roles of spiritual and political leadership.

Surprising Roles

These three women, Miriam, Deborah, and Huldah, are representative of the quite surprising roles some women have played during the centuries of Israel's history. We have selected these three women not only because of the strong roles they played, but because of the varied periods of time in which they lived.

Miriam was alongside Moses at the beginning stages of the history of Israel. Again, her sin of sibling rivalry and jealousy should not cause us to lose perspective of the significant role of leadership she did have.

Deborah's career was during the premonarchy period of the judges, a time of chaos and wantonness in Israel's history. During this time God raised up charismatic leaders who would be heroic deliverers from oppression and forces for stable leadership in perilous days. We believe it is significant indeed that one of the major judges was a woman. When we compare her with Samson, whose phenomenal physical strength was compromised by moral and character weakness, or with Gideon, whose early faith was like a bud yet to bloom, Deborah's story is all the more remarkable.

Finally, we are impressed with the story of Huldah. She was a true prophetess of Yahweh during the period of th⁞ late monarchy, a time when the full force of Israel's patriarchy was felt.

In the Ideal

That some significant women have conspicuous places of leadership and serve as examples of vitality in the life of the Old Testament period, however, is not the major point. We believe that what is most important is that in the *realm of the ideal*, women may have a prominent role to play beyond, but not excluding, the home. It is in this regard that we return to the passage that is so often cited, but so rarely stressed in this manner, Proverbs 31.

Proverbs 31:10-31 should not be read to discourage a woman, but to encourage us all. The picture in this climax of biblical wisdom is of a person of worth. Her portrait is not a template against which to mark our failures, but an ideal that opens doors of opportunities for all women of worth.

When a woman sees her life in the context of the noble woman of Proverbs 31, she sees her life as under the blessing of God:

> Give her the reward she has earned,
> and let her works bring her praise at the city gate
> (Proverbs 31:31).

Chapter 9, Notes

1. Darlene Craig, *A Worthy Woman: "Her Price Is Far Above Rubies" Proverbs 31:10-31* (Salem, Ore.: Valor Press, 1983); Jill Briscoe, *Queen of Hearts: The Role of Today's Woman, Based on Proverbs 31* (Old Tappan, N.J.: Fleming H. Revell, 1984); and Marsha Drake, *The Proverbs 31 Lady, And Other Impossible Dreams* (Minneapolis: Bethany House Publishers, 1984).

2. "Ruby," words by Cynthia Clawson and Raymond Brown. Copyright 1983 by Triune Music, Inc. and Charlie Monk Music. Used by permission.

3. Cited by Ellen Goodman, "Superwoman, Supertired" (December 1979), in *At Large*, copyright 1981 by the Washington Post Company. Reprinted by permission of Summit Books, a division of Simon & Schuster, Inc.

4. Ibid., 63.

5. A theme developed by Ronald B. Allen, *The Majesty of Man: The Dignity of Being Human* (Portland, Ore.: Multnomah Press, 1984), 153-70.

6. The Mosaic Law had some limitations on a married woman's freedom in making vows (religious and financial), presumably because her own actions might imperil her husband, without her ability to make good on these vows on her own. See Numbers 30. It is obvious, however, that a working wife today has as fully the ability as her husband to make good on her financial obligations. We reject as culturally insensitive those approaches to Numbers 30 that would restrict a contemporary working wife from having her own VISA card!

7. Nancie Carmichael speaks of Bible studies as one of America's greatest strengths. "Why Bible Studies?" *Virtue*, September/October 1982, 41.

8. Dee Jepsen, *Beyond Equal Rights* (Waco, Tex.: Word Books, 1984), 50.

9. Ibid., 114.

10. Lynda Johnson Robb, Foreword to Anne Bowen Follis, *I'm Not a Women's Libber, But . . .; And Other Confessions of a Christian Feminist*, (Nashville: Abingdon Press, 1981), 11. The well-known daughter of President Johnson continues: "Despite the fact that I grew up in the public eye, when I graduated from college I felt that what I wanted most to do was marry, care for my children, and manage my household. Clearly that has paid off in the richness of my life with my husband and my children. Like Anne, I have come to understand it is that richness which makes it possible and necessary for me to work for full equality for women. For women and men were created equal by God, and must become so in the eyes of the law of this land."

11. We may point to *Partnership*, the new magazine designed especially for pastors' wives to help them balance their personal and ministry lives; an excellent and provocative publication.

12. This is a point made by Kau respecting life in colonial New England. "Generally, when feminists speak of a patriarchy, they do so with scorn, implying that women are dominated entirely by men and are totally oppressed. In many patriarchal societies this is not at all the case and was not in rural New England. Patriarchy is not rule by men. It is rule by the father whose power is often shared with the mother. Mothers enjoy, in a agrarian society, a powerful position within the home as producers of not only children but also all kinds of goods necessary for sustaining life." (Ina J. Kau, "Feminists in the American Evangelical Movement" [master's thesis, Pacific School of Religion, Berkeley, 1977], 27.)

When God created man,
he made him in the likeness of God.
He created them male and female;
at the time they were created,
he blessed them and called them "man."
Genesis 5:1-2

Conclusion

The headline of a recent article on America's space program is a mark of our times: "'We've Come a Long Way,' Woman Astronaut Says."[1] The story was about Judy Resnik who followed Sally Ride in bringing American women into prominence in mankind's quest for destiny in the space age. Resnik was suggesting a great deal more than just the campaign slogan for a brand of cigarettes. Women have indeed come a long way in the last two decades. The new excitement in the space program is not just in technology; it is in people: *women* now join men in one of mankind's greatest adventures.

Women in the House . . . and the Senate

Women are joining men in many endeavors much nearer the ground as well. An increasing number of women may be found in significant leadership positions in giant corporations as well as in running their own small businesses at home. Women are now excelling in the professions as well as continuing to serve their communities in volunteer work. Women have gained increasingly high positions in government service and continue to meet many needs in education and other more traditional work roles.[2]

Some of these new career women are single, but many are married—and a great number are mothers. In the flight of the space shuttle *Discovery* in November 1984, Anna Fisher became the first mother to fly in space. Working mothers (that is, mothers who work outside their homes!) constitute a major phenomenon of change in our society which culture at large and the church as well are still trying to understand and accept.

201

Facing Change

Sometimes the enormity of the changes is hard to hold in perspective. An ad in a recent magazine still startles us. The banner read "Mother's Work," and the ad pictured a pregnant woman in a tailored jacket worn over a dress with a bow at the neck. The ad copy stated, "pregnant executives—classic business suits and dresses, conservatively styled for a professional image throughout pregnancy." It was not too long ago pregnant women were expected to be "in confinement."

A century ago in this country, a mother's work centered in the home; her daily crises did not include preparing a brief to argue a case before the Supreme Court nor acting upon a new corporate acquisition. More likely, the woman of an earlier age faced the type of domestic situation comedy described by Shirley Abbott in her story, "The Horrors of Housekeeping in 1855." The epic in this story is the demand upon the woman to get the noonday meal done on time, with everything hot at once. This is not easy even today; over a hundred years ago it was nearly impossible—especially for a young wife.

The Clock Strikes One

Fanny Van Courtlandt was twenty; she was being aided by her household servant Rosey, sixteen. After doing what she thought was everything, Fanny realized she still had not started the coffee. At that moment four events happened: the clock struck one, a rapping on the back door announced the iceman, Rosey screamed, and the Van Courtlandt men came down the kitchen stairs—Uncle Henry first.

Fanny was stripped to her corset because of the difficulty of working long so near the wood stove. Rosey was supposed to remind her to put her dress on before one—but she had forgotten! Fanny grabbed her garments and tried to hide her embarrassment behind a chair. To the end of her days she remembered the five faces: the astounded iceman, the horrified Uncle Henry, her chalk-white husband Charles, and her cousin Samuel—a little too amused for his own good. And there was Rosey—dabbing her eyes with her stained apron.[3]

The Journey

Women have come a long way. But not all of that way has proved to be good,[4] and not all women have participated on the journey. Further, how much of the journey has been the road to self-fulfillment only, and how much to finding fulfillment in reflecting the majesty of the Creator? Elaine Stedman puts the journey in perspective: "No one has arrived—we're all on a journey. We have a mutual destiny: to be conformed to the image of Christ—HIS image, not ours!"[5] This is a missing step in the walk of far too many women—and men—in our new day.

The center of life is in one's relationship to the Lord Jesus Christ. A far more important evaluation of success than achievement in one's career will be in how well a woman—or a man—reflects the person of Jesus. How much one is a mirror of the Maker. How much one's lifestyle reveals the wisdom of God.

Blessed Together

God created man as male and female to mirror his majesty, to reflect his beauty, and to rule together in the universe he has made.

Yet everything possible has been done to destroy God's plan for man. All the powers of darkness are concentrated on causing man to break the mirror, shatter the image, and increase his alienation from God.

In our day the energy of the evil one seems particularly concentrated on keeping men and women from working together to mirror their Maker. Forces for change are pitted against forces for traditionalism. Confusion reigns.

In this postfall world we mirror our Creator in distorted ways. At times we are like a mirror whose silver backing is corroded; the reflected image is barely perceptible. At other times we are like the mirrors in a carnival fun house, drastically distorting the reality of the one reflected.

The contemporary women's movement is a social force with the potential for incalculable evil. In its more radical forms it portends the end of the family and a nightmarish perversion of Eden—an Orwellian parody of paradise in which no male/

female distinction exists. Certainly there is no blessing from God in such a world.

Against such perversions we join with James Dobson in his warning, "self-awareness begins with an understanding of our own sexual identity. It must not be blurred by the forces of revolution raging around us."[6]

It was, after all, as *male* and *female* that God created us.

At the same time the women's movement is a social force the Spirit of God may use to cause men and women to reevaluate how they relate to one another, and to encourage true biblical values:

- Treating one another as full human beings
- Respecting one another as coheirs of God's gift of life
- Sharing with one another all the dignity, nobility, and wonder God invested in us at the beginning
- Ruling God's earth together as well as filling it

No more Archie Bunkerisms.

No more demeaning of women.

Much more of Jesus—in whose presence women and children had equal access with men.

Women and men who have their identity in the Lord Jesus Christ have the most at stake in the modern revolution, for we also care the most. It is we who believe that man as male and female was made in God's image. It is we who believe that our genuine humanity is to be rediscovered in Jesus Christ. It is we who believe that a biblical balance concerning man as male and female is God's intention for us all.

None should care as much about male and female issues as the Christian.

As we have worked on this book together we have had many opportunities to reflect upon our own relationship. It is a relationship of strength. It is also a relationship of weakness. We are by no means the perfect couple with the perfect marriage to mirror God. But we desire to improve what we have in our marriage to reflect Christ to others more clearly. We desire to polish the mirror of our relationship and have it be a more true reflection of our Creator.

As we live on this side of the coming Kingdom of the Lord Jesus Christ on earth, all of us have to ask what kind of world we wish for ourselves and for our children. As salt and light in an age of decay and darkness, we need to work for that kind of world. But we also need to work as parents, as partners, as persons in the spheres God has given to each of us.

The choices are ours to make, as the Spirit may empower us. Let us mirror him together.

Conclusion, Notes

1. Howard Benedict, "'We've Come a Long Way,' Woman Astronaut Says," Associated Press story, *The [Portland] Oregonian*, 20 June 1984.

2. We are well aware that this paragraph will cause some readers to bristle. Inequities still exist; pay scales are still uneven; there are still many barriers to women and to people of color for many positions. We will leave the campaign slogans to Judy Goldsmith, current president of NOW, however, and let our general remarks stand.
Following the assassination of Indira Gandhi (31 October 1984), only Great Britain (Prime Minister Margaret Thatcher) and Yugoslavia (President Milka Planinc) presently are led by women. But strides are being made by women in national governments in a number of countries, particularly in Scandinavia. Elisabeth Kopp is the first woman ever elected to the Swiss cabinet. In time she is expected to serve as the president of Switzerland. (Abigail Trafford, "Women's Impact Spreads in Global Politics," *US News & World Report*, 12 November 1984, 37-38.)

3. Shirley Abbott, "The Horrors of Housekeeping in 1855," *Smithsonian*, August 1984, 93.

4. "Along with the gains women have made in U. S. society during the past decade has come one glaring negative: more are breaking the law. . . . Arrests of women for serious offenses jumped nearly 20 percent in the last 10 years, compared with a 13.3 percent rise for men. In all, women account for about 20 percent of arrests each year." (Ted Gest, "Women Expand Their Roles in Crime, Too," *US News & World Report*, 12 November 1984, 62.

5. Elaine Stedman, *A Woman's Worth* (Waco, Tex.: Word Books, 1980), 40.

6. James Dobson, "A New Look at Masculinity & Femininity," *Moody Monthly*, June 1982, 54.

Scripture Index

Subject Index

in broadcast media, 17, 18, 26n

brutalizing of, 76

and careers, 19-20, 39

celebration of, 114-15

ceremonies for, 156

childbearing of, 122-24

Christian perspective, 69-70

church leadership, 80, 83n

clothing restraints, 36, 39

in college, 19, 189

in colonial New England, 198n

and culture, 34

demeaning attitudes toward, 15-21, 93, 101, 204

desire of, 124

dress modestly, 148-49

equality with husband, 89-103, 106, 115-17, 137, 146

family relationships, 80

free to be themselves, 28

gifted and able to contribute, 76

growing up female, 17-18

heresy in, 153n

hope in God, 173

and housework, 37, 38, 191

husband-hunting, 19

ideal, 197

identity in children and family, 84n

inferior to men? 75

in Judaism, 104n

Kikuyu, 48-49

in leadership, 100, 192, 193-97, 201

learning to be stupid, 17-18

in ministry, 84n

missionaries, 20

and Nazirite vow, 159

options open to, 184

ordination of, 71-76, 83-84n

in pastoral roles, 83n

personal growth, 184

piety of, 185

"place in the home," 68, 69, 192

praying and prophesying, 147

preaching/teaching, 20, 72-73, 76, 162

pursuit of dignity for, 21, 22

radical groups, 42n

rebellious, 74

in religious studies, 50

in Scripture, 155-75

in space program, 201

speaking in church, 145-49

spirituality ideals, 163

submission of, 72-73, 81, 124-27, 145-49, 173

teaching children, 73-74

voices of, 17, 26n

volunteer activities, 191-92

and the vote, 20, 41

as weaker sex, 123, 173

as wife and mother, 38

and the womb, 31, 33, 99

work and home, 182-85

worldview of, 187

in worship, 145-49, 152n

Women's liberation

See Feminism, Women's movement

Women's movement

base: dignity and worth, 30

diversity in, 30-31

Jewish women in, 21

nineteenth century, 84n

options in, 186

potential for evil or good, 203-204

quest for dignity, 21, 30

See Feminism

Women's Strike for Equality, 41

Worship and women, 145-49, 152n

Yahweh, 107-8, 127n

Yentl, 71, 83n

Zelophehad's daughters, 65, 70-71, 82